Cultivating a Sustainable Mindset in Finance

Mobilising the Capital Needed to Combat Climate Change

By
Danyelle Guyatt

Cultivating a Sustainable Mindset in Finance: Mobilising the Capital Needed to Combat Climate Change
By Danyelle Guyatt

This book first published 2023
Ethics International Press Ltd, UK
British Library Cataloguing in Publication Data
A catalogue record for this book is available from the British Library

Print Book ISBN: 978-1-80441-066-0
eBook ISBN: 978-1-80441-067-7

Contents

Foreword

I grew up in what Norwegian eco-philosopher Sigmund Kwaloy calls the Industrial Growth Society. This era sees the Earth as an endless source, and as an undamageable system capable of self-recovery. The mindset of the Industrial Growth Society values growth and expansion. The period started over two hundred years ago, when we realized that we could figure out how to be more productive by streamlining processes and automating them. Productivity meant lower costs and more profits. Capital was able to generate more capital, and progress equaled growth. Having more, and having it sooner were good goals.

Alas, there were other characteristics of this mindset. The ever-expanding need for resources came with expansions of global corporations, military interventions, and occupations. The mantra of the 1980s – "greed is good", nurtured individualistic, hedonistic behaviors benefiting the elites. Globalization helped to foster consumerism, in a spiral of increasing use of natural resources, extraction and depletion, with negative social, health and wellbeing impacts. Caught in a sum-zero logic, the choice was between planet or profit, and from the perspective of the short-term, profit won.

Of course, there were challenges and obstacles, but it was possible to look away, complaining about politicians, corporations, 'lazy people' or 'the system'[1]. All in all, it was easy to live in self-contained bubbles, enjoying this micro-stable worldview, where we thought we had figured things out: we had science, technology, and infinite human ingenuity to create progress, growth, better standards of living, comfort, and access to goods, longer lives and globalization to have it all.

The illusion didn't last, and we can think of the holes in the ozone layer as a physical representation of the holes in our paradigm: the beneficiaries of progress were a rather small percentage of the population, while the costs of the extended party were carried mostly by those who didn't participate in, nor benefitted from much of that progress. Certainly, voices had started to rise already in the second half of the past century, pointing at early signals of the consequences of the unsustainable paradigm we had collectively adopted. Some studied the extinction of species, CO2 levels in the atmosphere, land and water ecosystems, pollution, degradation of soils, the use of chemicals, nuclear proliferation, and waste. With access to the Internet, social injustice and inequity also became exposed, even within well structured global supply chains. Many questionable or unethical behaviors had lasted because they had been hidden and unquestioned. The Internet shrank and connected the world, making it transparent for all to see. Good people doing bad things were confronted and exposed to the gap between their values and their behaviors.
That the micro-stable worldview was based on un-sustainable foundations may have not been obvious to its main players, until disruptive weather events impacted the life of individuals independently of their geographical location.

---

[1] Growing up in Argentina, the conservative and right-wing people used to see social divide and poverty as self-inflicted ills, because the poor "were lazy". The progressives and leftists blamed corporations and "the system".

Some called this "the Great Unraveling". I call it the bursting of the micro-stable paradigm bubble, and it brought an increasing sense of urgency to do something, to address the challenges, find solutions, and innovate our way out of the problems we are facing.

But, as Einstein famously observed, we cannot solve a problem from within the thinking that created it. In other words, as Danyelle Guyatt intelligently notes, it may be time to revise the mindset that brought us here, and to develop a more functional, resilient, and effective mindset for sustainability. Certainly, developing a mindset sounds like a complex, if not impossible task. However, Danyelle shows in this book that it may be easier than we imagine.

As the developer of the Sustainability Mindset Principles framework, I have been asked which of the twelve principles is the most important. My answer is: start with the principle of Purpose. I recall a conversation with a pioneering business leader, who had built a solid and well branded organic coffee roasting company. Towards the end of our interview, I asked him what advice he had for educators who were interested in developing a generation of leaders more conscious of the planet and people. After reflecting in silence for a few moments, he replied: I wish someone had asked me, when I was in college, what my purpose was, why I was doing what I was doing. I probably wouldn't have had an answer at that time, but I would have started my journey of seeking the answer many decades ago, not when I was in my 50s.

As you go through the thought-provoking pages of this book, I invite you, the reader, to occasionally pause and ask yourself:

What is my purpose? Why am I doing the work I'm doing? What is the difference I want to make in the world? What ancestor am I being for the generations to come? You may not have the answer at this time, but it may start you on a journey of pursuit of meaning that you will never regret.

Isabel Rimanoczy, Ed.D,. Co-Founder and Director of SMindicator LLC
Fort Lauderdale, July 2023

Introduction

The world is waking up to the realisation that there is an imbalance in the global ecosystem that requires urgent attention and action from governments, corporations, investors, and civil society. Many of us are all too aware that humans have been placing extreme pressure on the planetary boundaries since the industrial revolution, resulting in increasingly unstable and extreme weather, loss of natural habitat and biodiversity and the growing risk of mass species extinction, including of the humankind.

While scientists, civil society activists, sustainability advocates and international organisations and policy makers have been echoing these concerns and making efforts to raise global action, it is only in recent years that the mainstream corporate and finance communities have begun to take the situation more seriously. A plethora of corporate statements, commitments and in some cases, real action, have surfaced as the powerful players in the global economy have increasingly realised that sustainability is not just about 'good' business, cost savings or competitive advantage; it is about the security, harmony, integrity, and viability of the entire global ecosystem that we have all co-created and depend on for our existence.

The question remains as to whether this 'waking up' is sufficiently strong and backed up by real action to avoid catastrophic outcomes in the short window of time that we have left. Many commentators have their doubts, including myself. Yet hope remains, and I remain on the side of hope, with the caveat that the window of time to act is quickly closing.

This is why mindsets matter, as mindsets shape our inner world and ultimately how we behave. As humans we have the evidence, data, tools, technologies, and capabilities to take swift action to avert dangerous climate change outcomes, biodiversity and habitat loss and ecological crises. What we don't have at the individual and societal level is the mindset that prevails over any perceived barriers to act with the urgency that is required. When we have a shared purpose to move to a more sustainable world, clarity in our beliefs and a determination to leverage our sphere of influence (both individually and in collaboration with others), then we can swiftly shift the global ecosystem onto a sustainable trajectory. Sustainability then becomes integral to our daily activities of community and family life, our work, research, teaching or business interests. In other words, cultivating a sustainability mindset means that we undergo an internal shift, such that our behaviour will naturally become more aligned with sustainability actions and outcomes.

I write this book from the perspective of an insider in the financial sector, which is why I am focusing on the cultivation of a sustainable mindset in finance. Having been academically trained and employed as an economist, financial strategist and investment consultant in the earlier stages of my working life, I understand the framework that many who work inside the financial sector may feel constrained to act within. The industry norms subconsciously lead to a certain way of thinking and behaving, as financial outcomes, personal advancement, bonuses, and the desire to simply 'fit in' to the culture is digested by recruits, new and old. A narrative unfolds and envelopes, as do industry conventions that serve to reinforce beliefs around the purpose of the financial sector, and the role that we each individually and collectively play.

The good news is that these norms and perceived binds are being challenged, unpicked, re-examined and – when beneficial – discarded and replaced with an approach that is more in tune with addressing the sustainability challenges of our time.

I had this realisation about a decade into my working life, when I was working for an investment bank in London and saw first-hand that the framework that the finance industry was working within had quite significant limitations in its real-life applicability. I was only in my late 20s and had already seen more than half a dozen large scale financial crises in different parts of the world, and as a strategist it was my job to try to make sense of these events and explain them to clients whose money we were managing. I saw that the constructs of rationality, portfolio diversification and market efficiency were just that, constructs rather than reality.

For one thing, there are many unrealistic assumptions about human behaviour that simply do not hold up to scrutiny when you observe how investors make decisions on a day-to-day basis. We are so much more complex than neoclassical theory would like us to believe. Yes, financial return is at the centre of what we do, but we are also human beings with emotions, biases, cognitive limitations, psychological processes, and social conformity pressures that impact on our daily decisions, and hence impact on how the financial system functions and serves the needs of society more broadly.

With a sustainable mindset, people who lead and work inside financial organisations have the potential to step back from the dominant narrative and look inward to reflect on what really matters to them in their personal and professional capacity, and indeed what matters to the organisation. The purpose and culture of organisations and the entire financial sector has the capacity to adapt and internalise sustainability into how it functions; it simply requires an individual and collective mindset shift, and the genuine sustainability actions that reflect that mindset shift will follow.

Obviously not all individuals or organisations will necessarily see the need or benefit of shifting towards a sustainable mindset, as it will require a certain level of introspection, investigation, and commitment that not everyone will be willing to undertake. The purpose of this book is not to replace one mantra with another, to present another 'rulebook' that is externally imposed by an outside entity, it is rather to invite readers to consider how their mindset interacts with their broader sustainability goals, and how these can be brought together in greater unison.

This book begins by exploring the role of the financial sector in helping to avert the social and ecological challenges of our time. We explore why mindsets matter, and why it is important for the financial sector to cultivate a sustainable mindset. The book builds on the emerging literature on sustainable mindsets and presents a framework to cultivate a sustainable mindset in the financial sector, with the emphasis on 'framing' the potential pathway rather than prescribing a one-size-fits-all solution.

This framework looks at the role of emotions (how we feel), cognition (how we think) and behaviour (what we do) in shaping the decisions that investors make on a day-to-day basis. Some of the qualities of a sustainable mindset that are particularly relevant for the financial sector includes embracing a broader sense of purpose in serving the needs of others, and a realisation and alignment of beliefs with that purpose in mind. Developing systems thinking and recognising the limits to growth and what the need for regeneration means for capital allocation decisions now and into the future is a core part of the mindset shift that is needed. When each investor can envision the future world and their role in creating that outcome, then there will be greater synergy between what they do on a day-to-day basis and achieving that long term vision.

We then look at the important role that the financial sector could play in closing the climate financing gap, as well as the informational and behavioural barriers to act, drawing from relevant literature and research evidence. The sustainable mindset framework is applied to the specific challenge of increasing capital allocation into activities that will help to close the climate financing gap. While this is not the only issue where the financial sector could play a pivotal role, it is evident that there is a persistent gap between the financing needs to mitigate and adapt to climate change that needs to be closed with greater urgency than we are currently witnessing. We show that a modest shift in our mindset could help to accelerate the financial flows into climate financing, with some practical suggestions provided to help achieve that shift.

1. The role of the finance sector in achieving sustainable development

"Saving our planet, lifting people out of poverty, advancing economic growth... these are one and the same fight. We must connect the dots between climate change, water scarcity, energy shortages, global health, food security, and women's empowerment. Solutions to one problem must be solutions for all."
Ban Ki-moon, former Secretary-general of the United Nations

"The financial sector lies at the front of the industrial value chain and should set and apply responsible finance guidelines that help mitigate adverse environmental practices. It should use its financial influence to expedite the value chain's transition to sustainability."
World Economic Forum (2023)

"Achieving the objective of the Paris Agreement to limit global temperature increases to 1.5°C from pre-industrial levels requires a whole economy transition. Every company, bank, insurer, and investor will need to adjust their business models, develop credible plans for the transition to a low-carbon, climate-resilient future, and then implement those plans."
Glasgow Financial Alliance for Net Zero (2021)

Defining the finance sector

The finance sector is predominantly comprised of retail banks, investment banks, development banks, non-bank financial institutions, insurance companies, pension funds, superannuation funds, mutual funds, investment managers, sovereign wealth funds, charities and endowments. In aggregate, the value of the assets that these groups collectively oversee as measured by the combined value of equity-market capitalization, corporate loans, bonds and global private markets was estimated to be worth in excess of US$480 trillion in 2021 (Statista, 2023). The financial sector presides over a large pool of capital, bringing with it significant power and influence over how the financial system functions and ultimately, the sustainability of the global ecosystem which we are all part.

The purpose of the financial sector

At its most fundamental level, the financial sector's functions are to provide safekeeping of financial assets, to allow individuals and organisations to transact with one another, to insure risk and to "intermediate" between lender and borrower (London Business School, n.d.). The financial sector impacts on the real economy through the savings and investments of the national income accounts of every nation, as well as through the allocation of capital for the purposes of production or investment (North and Buckley, 2010). The sector collectively influences the price and value of assets, market liquidity, the cost of capital and where capital is allocated, as well as the stability, fairness, and equity of the financial system. The financial sector therefore plays a central role in enabling and financing the shift towards a more sustainable and inclusive global economy (World Economic Forum, 2023).

As this chapter highlights, there are positive indications that the financial sector is aware of the challenges posed by climate change and the benefits of sustainable development, reversing biodiversity loss and restoring balance in our ecosystem. We will see that many financial institutions are collaborating on a raft of sustainability issues; they are making pledges to achieve net zero by 2050 and support the Sustainable Development Goals (SDGs), including climate justice and poverty alleviation. Yet at the same time we are seeing a proliferation in litigation cases, rising accusations of greenwashing, continued financing of expansion in fossil fuel extraction activities and an alarming persistence in the climate financing gap.

We are at a critical junction in redressing the sustainability issues of our time, and the financial sector plays a crucial role in that process. We need to revisit the core purpose of the finance sector, and how that relates to addressing some of the market failings that are giving rise to the global sustainability challenges that we face. The core functions / purpose of the financial sector and how these relate to sustainable development are summarised below.

a) **Broader sense of purpose and serving others.** The existence of the financial sector is fundamentally based on allocating capital to where it will best serve society, be it helping families buy a home or saving for retirement; helping businesses raise capital to support growth and employment; and helping people manage risks and prepare for a rainy day (IMF, 2019). Reconnecting back to the fundamental purpose of financial service to serve others opens pathways to see how the financial sector can be a 'force for good' (Force for Good, n.d.) as part of carrying out its activities, where individual responsibility is grounded in values and ethics, and a sense of personal responsibility to do the right thing.

This fundamental purpose – to serve others – is integral to the process of generating financial returns and profits and not separate to it, where money and morals co-exist (Sandel, 2013), building the strong foundation for exercising duty of care and building societal trust in a sector that is integral to the quality of everyone's lives and the environment in which we all live (Waitzer and Sarro, 2014).

b) **Efficient allocation of resources.** The ultimate function of the financial sector is not to speculate over future movements in asset prices to maximise short-term financial returns, but rather to allocate capital to the most beneficial activities for society over the long-term (Stracca, 2004). Allocative efficiency is therefore about how well the financial sector allocates capital to where it is most needed, taking into account consumer's preferences and needs. Evidently with the growing realization and acknowledgement that planetary health and human health and well-being are interdependent, the financial system can facilitate the efficient allocation of resources in a way that will be most beneficial for the economy, society and the environment in the long run. In this way, the capital requirements to close the financing gaps to achieve the Paris Agreement and the SDGs are central to the workings of the financial sector in terms of allocating capital to where it is most needed.

c) **Stability.** Central Banks and financial regulators recognise the risk that sustainability poses for the stability of the financial system, and have introduced a series of checks and balances, scenario analysis tools and reporting requirements based on the Task Force on Climate-related Financial Disclosures (TCFD) recommendations to ensure that the financial sector is adequately assessing, managing, and disclosing these risks (World Bank Group, 2017). The link between pension funds, insurers and banks in underpinning financial stability and safeguarding the wellbeing and safety of households and firms in the face of climate change and ecological imbalance is widely recognised (European Central Bank, 2019).

d) **Security and safety.** As part of fulfilling their role to provide a secure retirement future for end beneficiaries and members, a growing body of international public and private sector pension funds, mutual funds and superannuation funds have publicly supported the Net Zero by 2050 goal and the attainment of the SDGs by 2030. Insurance and reinsurance companies also play an important role in mitigating and adapting to the effects of climate change in both developed and emerging economies through how they invest their surplus capital, as well as the provision of insurance products and services to help communities manage and mitigate climate-related risks. There is potential for the financial sector to escalate its influence over the companies and entities in which it invests, to engage with governments to promote accelerated policy measures, and to increase the allocation of capital to activities that enable and accelerate climate mitigation, resilience and sustainable development (OECD, 2021).

Highlight: Defining Sustainable Finance

While there is no universally agreed definition of sustainable finance, a widely cited definition is provided by the European Commission as part of its Sustainable Finance activities:

"Sustainable finance refers to the process of taking environmental, social and governance (ESG) considerations into account when making investment decisions in the financial sector, leading to more long-term investments in sustainable economic activities and projects."
Source: European Commission (2022)

To understand what this means in practice, we need to understand and define sustainable development, and what that entails for the financial sector. We also need to understand what ESG means and how that can be actioned in practice across the financial sector, as the terminology is still loosely defined. In addition, an understanding of how the finance sector functions, its role and the different participants in the financial sector are important to interpret what integrating ESG might involve for them.

A number of frameworks, standards, guidelines, and sustainability taxonomies have been developed in an attempt to consolidate what sustainability means and how it relates to the activities of the financial sector. It is widely noted that a clearer definition of sustainable finance will improve measurement and disclosure standards, which will help to reduce the risk of misleading statement or incomplete information in the market.

However, as this book argues, the internal conditions – that is the mindsets of the people inside the financial institutions, the culture of the industry and the 'rules of the game' at the market wide level have received far less attention than the external conditions have received (be it information gaps, regulations, or industry guidelines). To embed sustainability into how the financial sector functions in a holistic way, both the internal and external conditions need to be considered.

The pursuit of sustainable development

The Brundtland Commission (1987) defined sustainability as "meeting the needs of the present without compromising the ability of future generations to meet their own needs" (UN Brundtland Commission, 1987).

- Sustainable development calls for concerted efforts towards building an inclusive, sustainable and resilient future for people and planet.
- For sustainable development to be achieved, it is crucial to harmonize three core elements: economic growth, social inclusion and environmental protection. These elements are interconnected, and all are crucial for the well-being of individuals and societies.
- Eradicating poverty in all its forms and dimensions is an indispensable requirement for sustainable development. To this end, there must be promotion of sustainable, inclusive, and equitable economic growth, creating greater opportunities for all, reducing inequalities, raising basic standards of living, fostering equitable social development and inclusion, and promoting integrated and sustainable management of natural resources and ecosystems.

The advancement of sustainable development extended the global work under the auspice of the Millennium Development goals (UNDP, n.d.) to launch a sustainable development agenda in 2016, "Transforming Our World: The 2030 Agenda for sustainable development". The SDGs (UNDP, 2018) contain 17 goals and 169 targets. The SDGs form the framework for improving the lives of populations around the world and mitigating the hazardous man-made effects of climate change. SDG 13: Climate Action, calls for integrating measures to prevent climate change within development frameworks. SDG 14: Life Below Water, and SDG 15: Life on Land, also call for more sustainable practices in using the earth's natural resources.

The SDGs call for action by all stakeholders: governments, civil society, charities and endowments, academic institutions, as well as the corporate and financial sector, to promote prosperity while protecting the planet., and others. The goals recognize that ending poverty must go together with strategies that build economic growth and address a range of social needs including education, health, social protection, and job opportunities, while tackling climate change and environmental protection.

As we will see in the ensuing discussion, many financial institutions have embraced the importance of the SDGs and have made efforts to incorporate these into their investment strategies, although we will also see that this action is failing to redirect capital to where it is most needed to achieve the goals of the SDGs.

Highlight: Definition of Sustainable Development

Sustainable Development is defined by the UN as development that meets the needs of the present without compromising the ability of future generations to meet their own needs (UNDP, 2018).

1. Sustainable development calls for concerted efforts towards building an inclusive, sustainable and resilient future for people and planet.

2. For sustainable development to be achieved, it is crucial to harmonize three core elements: economic growth, social inclusion and environmental protection. These elements are interconnected and all are crucial for the well-being of individuals and societies.

3. Eradicating poverty in all its forms and dimensions is an indispensable requirement for sustainable development. To this end, there must be promotion of sustainable, inclusive and equitable economic growth, creating greater opportunities for all, reducing inequalities, raising basic standards of living, fostering equitable social development and inclusion, and promoting integrated and sustainable management of natural resources and ecosystems.

This goal gained the support of 193 Member States of the United Nations for a new sustainable development agenda, "Transforming Our World: The 2030 Agenda for sustainable development". This agenda contains 17 goals and 169 targets.

Sustainability criteria: In this report reference to "sustainability criteria" includes the environmental, social and governance (ESG) factors that will support the attainment of sustainability goals (PRI, n.d.). There are currently no agreed standardized sustainability criteria at the international level, although there are differing standards and emerging practices that are being applied.

Climate change as a systemic risk

Climate change is a threat to human well-being and planetary health, and the window of opportunity to secure a liveable and sustainable future for all is rapidly closing. The goal of the Paris Agreement to "limit global warming to well below 2°C and pursue efforts to limit the temperature increase to 1.5°C compared to the pre-industrial age" requires escalated action and prioritisation by governments, businesses, investors and civil society (WMO, 2023). The financial sector invests into the global economy and is thus not immune or outside of the systemic risks posed by climate change. Indeed, as the IPCC (2023) noted in the Synthesis Report of the Sixth Assessment Report, the financial sector plays a critical role in helping to steer the global economy to a more sustainable footing through its financing decisions.

The IPCC (2023) reported that the pace and scale of climate change is manifesting more quickly and is more extreme and damaging than previous assessments indicated. IPCC explained that the choices and actions implemented in this decade will have impacts now and for thousands of years. Building climate resilience requires an escalation in action and investment in adaptation and mitigation activities, to reduce the projected losses and damages for humans and ecosystems. Such investment will also deliver many co-benefits, such as improved air quality and health. Further delays in mitigation and adaptation action will lock-in high-emissions infrastructure, increase the risks of stranded assets and significantly increase losses and damage costs.

This calls for a whole of sector, whole of economy and whole of society transition, to achieve deep and sustained emissions reductions and secure a liveable and sustainable future for all. A significant upscaling of a wide portfolio of mitigation and adaptation options is required, with feasible, effective, and low-cost options for mitigation and adaptation already available today. While government policy and technological development play a central role in supporting and escalating climate action, the IPCC (2023) also highlighted the critical role that the financial sector plays in enabling the accelerated climate action through how it allocates capital.

More specifically, the IPCC noted that if climate goals are to be achieved, both adaptation and mitigation financing would need to increase many-fold. While there is sufficient global capital to close the global investment gaps, the IPCC observed that there are barriers that are slowing down the redirection of capital towards mitigation and adaptation activities that need to be urgently addressed.

> The focus of this book is to examine the perceived barriers to unlocking the capital that is needed to finance the mitigation and adaptation activities, which the IPCC identified as being critical for building climate resilience and securing a liveable and sustainable future for all.

Environmental, Social, and Governance (ESG) issues

The financial sector has become increasingly aware of the important role that it plays in shaping the way the global financial system functions, and how its activities impact on society and the environment more broadly. This has given rise to several industry-led developments, one of which was the emergence of the UN backed Principles for Responsible Investment (PRI). It was established in 2006 after the then United Nations Secretary-General Kofi Annan invited a group of the world's largest institutional investors to join a process to develop the PRI, whose mission is defined as follows:

> *"We believe that an economically efficient, sustainable global financial system is a necessity for long-term value creation. Such a system will reward long-term, responsible investment and benefit the environment and society as a whole.*
>
> *The PRI will work to achieve this sustainable global financial system by encouraging adoption of the Principles and collaboration on their implementation; by fostering good governance, integrity and accountability; and by addressing obstacles to a sustainable financial system that lie within market practices, structures and regulation."*
> Source: PRI, www.unpri.org/about-us/about-the-pri

As part of the PRI's evolution, the terminology of Environmental, Social and Governance (ESG) emerged from a series of interactions between international sustainable investment specialists, and six Principles for Responsible Investment were created. At the time of writing in February 2023, there were over 3,800 signatories to the PRI, representing asset owners (pension funds, superannuation funds, insurance companies, charities and endowments), asset managers (investment managers), and service providers (consultants, research and data providers) with a combined US$121 trillion in assets under management.

In this book, reference to "sustainability" includes the environmental, social and governance (ESG) issues that will support the attainment of the sustainability goals.

The somewhat perplexing aspect of the PRI is that while signatories make a commitment to the PRI and agree to abide by the six principles which centre around integrating ESG into investment processes, there is no definitive list of ESG issues, and no intention to develop any such list. Rather, the PRI produces examples of ESG issues, and leave investors to undertake the assessments needed as it relates to their investment portfolios. The list provided by the PRI is reproduced in Figure 1.

Figure 1.

ESG Issue	Examples
Environmental (E)	Issues relating to the quality and functioning of the natural environment and natural systems. These include biodiversity loss; greenhouse gas (GHG) emissions, climate change, renewable energy, energy efficiency, air, water or resource depletion or pollution, waste management, stratospheric ozone depletion, changes in land use, ocean acidification and changes to the nitrogen and phosphorus cycles.
Social (S)	Issues relating to the rights, well-being and interests of people and communities. These include human rights, labour standards in the supply chain, child, slave and bonded labour, workplace health and safety, freedom of association and freedom of expression, human capital management and employee relations; diversity; relations with local communities, activities in conflict zones, health and access to medicine, HIV/AIDS, consumer protection; and controversial weapons.

ESG Issue	Examples
Governance (G)	Issues relating to the governance of companies and other investee entities. In the listed equity context these include board structure, size, diversity, skills and independence, executive pay, shareholder rights, stakeholder interaction, disclosure of information, business ethics, bribery and corruption, internal controls and risk management, and, in general, issues dealing with the relationship between a company's management, its board, its shareholders and its other stakeholders. This category may also include matters of business strategy, encompassing both the implications of business strategy for environmental and social issues, and how the strategy is to be implemented. In the unlisted asset classes governance issues also include matters of fund governance, such as the powers of Advisory Committees, valuation issues, fee structures, etc.

Source: www.unnpri.org

The commitment of signatories to the PRI sets out the alignment of ESG issues with acting in the best interests of beneficiaries and fiduciary duty and the performance of investment portfolios.

> *"As institutional investors, we have a duty to act in the best long-term interests of our beneficiaries. In this fiduciary role, we believe that environmental, social, and corporate governance (ESG) issues can affect the performance of investment portfolios (to varying degrees across companies, sectors, regions, asset classes and through time)."*
>
> *...We believe this will improve our ability to meet commitments to beneficiaries as well as better align our investment activities with the broader interests of society."*
> Source: www.unpri.org

The emphasis of the PRI is thus on the benefits of integrating ESG into investment processes for portfolio performance, rather than the wider positive real-world benefits of taking a more holistic approach to investing. While the latter part of the above statement recognises that ESG issues and the broader interests of society are in alignment, it falls short of acknowledging that investors could contribute to developing a financial system that can enable sustainable outcomes through how it functions and behaves.

There have been more recent developments in regard to impact investment and blended finance amongst PRI signatories and some workstreams that have opened up new conversations and perspectives for investors to align their investment decisions with an intention to also positively impact on the real-world. For example, a review was published in 2021 with the support of the PRI, UNEP FI and the Generation Foundation that indicated the legal frameworks across 11 different jurisdictions do allow investors to align their financial decisions with sustainability outcomes, as the two are, in effect, intertwined (PRI, 2021).

Nevertheless, positive impact goals are not embedded into the core principles of the PRI and positive impact is still considered to be a niche or 'additional' activity for purpose-led investors, rather than the mainstream investment community (PRI, 2019).

Investor pledges on Sustainable Development

The 2030 Agenda for Sustainable Development was adopted by all United Nations Member States in 2015, as a shared blueprint for peace and prosperity for people and the planet, now and into the future. The SDGs represent an urgent call for action by all countries - developed and developing - in a global partnership. The goals recognize that ending poverty and other deprivations must go hand-in-hand with strategies that improve health and education, reduce inequality, and spur economic growth – all while tackling climate change and working to preserve our oceans and forests. There are 17 SDGs and 169 individual targets that support the attainment of the SDGs by 2030 as summarised in Figure 2.

Figure 2.

The goals have resonated with many business leaders and financial institutions worldwide, as they provide the opportunity for the private sector to contribute to supporting a more sustainable, fair, and secure world (GRI et al, n.d.). This not only makes business sense in terms of providing a more stable environment for companies and investors to operate and invest into, but it also reinforces the powerful role that the private sector plays – alongside the public sector, NGOs and civil society – in shaping the direction and health of the global ecosystem.

Some financial institutions have embraced the SDGs to guide their decision-making process, as part of the growing effort to broaden the narrative and activities in relation to responsible investment towards 'enabling' sustainable outcomes (compared to 'alignment with'). This development and shift in narrative is subtle yet powerful, as it requires a wider acknowledgement of the interrelationship between the financial sector and environmental and social outcomes.

The SDGs also come at a time when investor appetite for greater transparency and disclosure is escalating, as evidenced by the widespread support for the Financial Stability Board's Task Force on Climate-Related Financial Disclosure recommendations (TCFD, 2017). Moreover, investor demand for greater alignment between financial goals and positive social and environmental outcomes is beginning to shift (Global Impact Investing Network, n.d.), reflecting changing societal expectations as well as greater awareness of the wider role that investors play in supporting a sustainable financial system (UNEP, 2017).

For example, in a conversation on the SDGs, the PRI noted that all actions by the financial sector have an impact on real world outcomes, and that the SDGs provide a useful framework for investors to consider such outcomes as an explicit part of the investment process (PRI, n.d.).

> *"Every action an investor takes shapes outcomes in the real world – whether they want it to or not.*
>
> *...This is a key time for investors to begin building their understanding of positive and negative outcomes – and to learn how they can shape those outcomes through their investment decisions, from their stewardship of investees and from their*

engagement with wider stakeholders such as policy makers. As the world's agreed goals for society and all its stakeholders, the SDGs provide a lens through which investors can align themselves with the needs of the wider world."

Source: Principles for Responsible Investment (2020)

This is quite a deviation from the consensus opinion within the PRI and the six agreed principles that guide the behaviour of its signatories. The fact that this debate has started and is being made public is a positive sign. It indicates that a shift is taking place in terms of how investors think about the relationship between their investment decisions and real-world outcomes that we can build on.

Investor commitments to achieve Net Zero by 2050

According to the IPCC, global Co2 emissions will need to decline by about 45% from 2010 levels by 2030 and reach net zero by around 2050 (IPCC, 2018). The IPCC projected that by 2100 global warming is projected to reach at least 3°C by 2100, with continued warming beyond that date, based on current commitments under the Paris Agreement (UNEP, 2022). In support of the goals of the Paris Agreement, there has been widespread adoption of a net zero emissions goal by 2050 (or earlier) across a range of actors including national, state and local governments, businesses, cities and investors, with commitments representing 1,049 cities, 67 regions, 5,235 businesses, 441 investors, and 1,039 Higher Education Institutions (UN Climate Change, 2022).

Despite these widespread commitments, as we will see later when we look at the problem of greenwashing and the persistent gap in the climate financing activities of the investment community, there is a gap between commitment and action that needs to be urgently addressed.

Figure 3. Number of national net zero pledges and share of global Co2 emissions covered

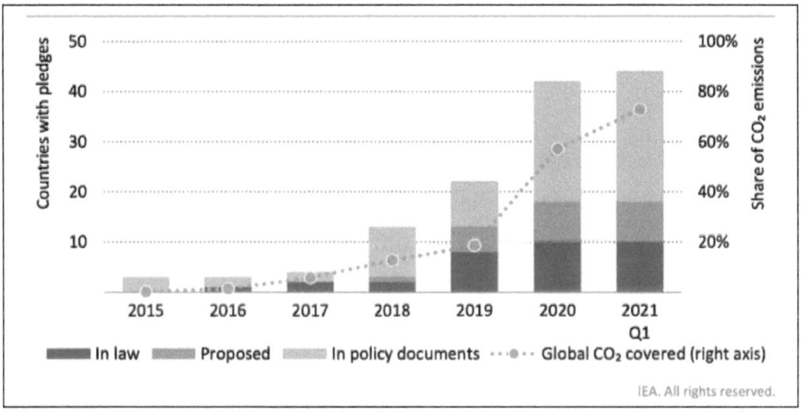

Source: IEA (2021)

Biodiversity loss

> *"Without nature, we are nothing. Nature is our life-support system, and yet humanity seems hell bent on destruction."*
> The UN Secretary-General, António Guterres

The Convention on Biological Diversity is dedicated to promoting sustainable development and was signed by 150 government leaders at the 1992 Rio Earth Summit. The Convention recognizes that "biological diversity is about more than plants, animals and micro-organisms and their ecosystems – it is about people and our need for food security, medicines, fresh air and water, shelter, and a clean and healthy environment in which to live" (UNEP, n.d.).

Up until recently, biodiversity loss has received much less attention from the financial sector compared to climate change. However, this is changing as the risks from biodiversity loss are increasingly being recognised. According to an OECD report, ecosystem services from biodiversity, such as crop pollination, water purification, flood protection and carbon sequestration, are worth an estimated US$125-140 trillion per year. About US$44 trillion per year of this global output is dependent on nature (Planet Tracker, 2022).

In 2021, participants in the financial sector launched an international initiative Taskforce on Nature-related Financial Disclosures (TFNFC, 2023). The aim to develop a risk management and disclosure framework for organizations to report and act on evolving nature-related financial risks, similar to the TCFD framework for climate-related financial disclosure.

The investor-led initiative – Nature Action 100 – builds on similar initiatives to help investors engage with companies that are contributing to biodiversity loss. Engaging with companies to reduce their negative impact on nature can be a powerful tool for change, especially when coming from large investors and asset owners.

Biodiversity is also attracting the attention of financial policymakers. In March 2022, the Network for Greening the Financial System published a statement (NGFS, 2023), acknowledging that biodiversity loss could lead to significant macroeconomic and financial stability risks.

Despite these positive developments, it is very early days in terms of the financial sector's involvement in financing biodiversity and allocating capital to support such goals. To illustrate this point, BloombergNEF (2023) estimated that $1 trillion per year is needed by 2030 to sustainably manage biodiversity, compared to $166 billion per annum currently.

Task force on Climate-related Financial Disclosure framework (TCFD)

The TCFD was established as an industry-led, multi-stakeholder process to improve financial disclosure around climate change including, but not limited to, an organisation's governance, strategy, risk management processes and utilisation of metrics/targets. The recommendations have received widespread attention, with more than 3,723 companies and 237 other organizations (e.g., industry associations, governments) with a combined market capitalization of $26 trillion (as reported in 2022). This includes over 1,500 financial institutions, responsible for assets of $220 trillion. In addition, as reported in 2022, 92 of the 100 largest public companies support the TCFD, report in line with the TCFD recommendations, or both (TCFD, 2022).

The financial sector is very much part of the TCFD implementation effort, with the PRI moving to incorporate the TCFD recommendations into its reporting framework for signatories. Indeed, the PRI has made the TCFD governance and strategy climate-related indicators mandatory for signatories to report since 2020. This underpins the need for investors and PRI signatories to be in alignment with the TCFD recommendations.
One of the expectations was that improved climate-related financial disclosure would promote more informed investment, credit, and insurance underwriting decisions, and increase the financing activities to support climate mitigation and adaptation. However,

it is now 5 years since the initial TCFD recommendations were released, and it is difficult to see any visible impact this has had on financing activities.

The TCFD (2022) undertook an annual review of progress for 2022 which highlighted that disclosure had improved considerably, that there was higher quality information available, and that there had been widespread support from the financial sector in requesting that companies (and themselves) report in alignment with the TCFD. However, increased information does not equate to increased investment. The TCFD reported that "climate-related risks are beginning to affect prices for certain types of assets" (TCFD, 2022:5), which is quite a vague and underwhelming outcome given the widespread acknowledgement of the urgency of the situation.

Sustainability taxonomies

Taxonomies are definitions of sustainability that aim to provide a comprehensive set of criteria for classifying finance, lending, investment and underwriting activities as having certain sustainability attributes. It can be used for bond issuance, portfolio and product development, providing a framework for labelling financial products as sustainable and promoting transparency and disclosure. while definitions of sustainable finance are less ambitious in scope (OECD, 2020 and ASFI, 2022).

As the OECD and others have observed, the potential benefits of sustainable finance definitions and taxonomies include:

- Improve market transparency, consistency and comparability about what sustainable finance is, and is not across different types of assets and jurisdictions.

- Reduce the risk of greenwashing by corporations and financial institutions by providing further clarity over classification of green and socially beneficial activities.

- Improve the confidence of retail investors to invest in sustainability labelled funds or companies.

- Encourage financial institutions to allocate capital to sustainable activities, to demonstrate their commitment to achieving stated goals, such as the attainment of the SDGs by 2030, a Just Transition and Net Zero by 2050 (as examples).

- Improve tracking of sustainable finance flows and the financing gap, such that policy makers and regulatory bodies can design appropriate policy measures and incentives to divert capital to where it is most needed to achieve sustainable development and alignment with the goals of the Paris Agreement.

According to ASFI (2022), there are 12 international taxonomies and a further 15 under development – collectively representing more than 55% of global GDP. While most of the taxonomies focus on environmental issues ("green"), there are also some emerging classifications that focus on "social" issues in the EU and China. Figure 4 highlight some of the features of the taxonomies across different jurisdictions.

Figure 4.

Taxonomy	Primary drivers
EU	Re-orienting capital flows toward sustainable investment and removing barriers to cross-border financing for sustainability projects. The taxonomy also serves as a reporting framework on climate-related disclosures.
UK	Tackling 'greenwashing' and setting a high bar globally with a rigorous, science-based taxonomy that helps accelerate green finance and support the UK's transition to a net zero economy.
China	Unifying standards of China's green bonds and providing greater harmonisation with global standards.
CGT	Facilitating interoperability and comparability of international taxonomies by providing a common language on sustainable finance definitions.
CBI	Providing an important resource for common green definitions across global markets, in a way that supports the growth of a cohesive thematic bond market that delivers a low carbon economy.
ASEAN	Facilitating interoperability and comparability of the various sustainable finance systems and policies in development by AMS.
Singapore	Facilitating the flow of capital to support the nation's transition to a low carbon economy and achieve its other environmental objectives.
Malaysia	Facilitating standardised classification and reporting of climate-related exposures to support risk assessments at the institution and systemic levels, strengthen accountability and market transparency and encourage financial flows towards supporting climate objectives.
Korea	Facilitating financial flows to green projects, providing an agreed-upon standard to control greenwashing and serving as a reference point for the financial sector in shifting investments from carbon-heavy industries towards more sustainable industries.
Japan	Directing more capital to support achieving the Paris Agreement by facilitating financing for climate transitions, especially in hard-to-abate sectors, and ensuring the credibility of "transition finance" labelling.
New Zealand	Improving the flow of sustainable finance to New Zealand's agricultural sector and supporting better on-farm sustainability outcomes
Canada	Aligning capital to credible transition pathways and climate objectives, with a focus on transition criteria for the mining sector.
Chile	Steering the market toward green projects, helping the government and financial institutions fulfil their climate goals and leading the global initiative for developing criteria for the mining sector.

Source: ASFI (2022)

While these efforts are a welcome development and will be beneficial in supporting consistency in terms of measurement and reporting in the long run, there are some red flags to consider regarding how much impact taxonomies and common definitions will have on capital flows into climate finance activities in the short window of time that we have remaining to address the climate crisis.

These red flags are further explored later in this book, but in brief, it takes a long time to develop the taxonomies, with some countries only just starting the process. If financing decisions are held back until these are final and agreed, we run the risk of not allocating capital at the scale and pace that is needed to 2030. There is also a lack of consistency in terms of the definitions across jurisdictions that makes it challenging for global investors to achieve comparability. Finally, there is the potential for self-interest and corporate / economic interference to water down the definitions within each jurisdiction.

Financial regulators and standard setting bodies

International standard setting bodies, central banks, prudential and financial regulators at the global and national level have expressed their widespread support for, and adoption of, the TCFD recommendations as a framework to improve disclosure around the material climate-related impacts for the organisations and entities within their jurisdictions. Some highlights of note:

- While the TCFD remains a voluntary, market-led initiative, many governments and regulators are taking steps to require or encourage disclosures based on the TCFD recommendations. Over 120 regulators and governments from around the world are TCFD supporters, including Belgium, Canada, Chile, Denmark, France, Ireland, Japan, New Zealand, Sweden, and the United Kingdom (UK) (TCFD, 2022).

- Central banks and supervisors from across the globe — through the Network for Greening the Financial System (Banque de France, 2019) — have encouraged companies issuing public debt or equity to disclose their investment practices and policies in alignment with the TCFD recommendations.

- In November 2021, the International Financial Reporting Standards Foundation announced the establishment of the International Sustainability Standards Board (ISSB), with the aim to develop a comprehensive global baseline of sustainability disclosure standards to meet investors' information needs. In March 2022, the ISSB published two exposure drafts for consultation. One sets out general sustainability- related disclosure standards and the other specifies climate-related disclosure standards. Both exposure drafts build upon the TCFD recommendations, with the latter covering elements of all 11 recommended disclosures.

- The Financial Stability Board published a stocktake of whether and how financial authorities incorporate climate-related risks into their financial stability monitoring (FSB, 2020). The FSB also stated its intention to conduct further work to assess the channels through which physical and transition risks could impact the financial system, and how they might interact.

- The UN Sustainable Stock Exchanges Initiatives launched a database that provides information on 78 stock exchanges that are taking actions to support enhancing climate- related financial disclosures in line with the TCFD recommendations in their markets. The most common action taken — by 50 stock exchanges — is providing TCFD training, followed by referencing the TCFD recommendations in the stock exchange's ESG disclosure guidance.

- In April 2022, the European Financial Reporting Advisory Group released the draft EU Sustainability Reporting Standards for public comment. The related disclosure requirements correspond to the pillars of the TCFD recommendations and ISSB standards.

While all these developments are important steps to create the institutional frameworks that support climate action, we will also see that they are focused primarily on addressing the external conditions that influence the corporate and financial sectors as they currently operate – that is, information, data, metrics, standards, best practice. In other words, there is little attention given to consider the 'internal' conditions that might be slowing down genuine action that no amount of data or information will address.

Questions that also need to be discussed, such as what assumptions are we collectively making about how the financial system works and how it can best serve the needs of society? What are the dominant paradigms that are embedded into our mental models and thinking, and are these still valid given the planetary boundaries that we are hitting? Without jumping too far ahead, we can begin to see that merely tweaking existing reporting and regulatory frameworks in response to a challenge that puts the entire ecosystem and survival at risk is not sufficient.

Fiduciary duty interpretation

As industry standards evolve across the institutional investment community and financial regulators continue to develop guidelines and frameworks, the management of sustainability issues is seen as being essential to trustees' fiduciary duty to act in the best financial interest of members (PRI, 2019a).

Fiduciary duties (or equivalent obligations) exist to ensure that those who manage other people's money act in the interests of the end beneficiaries, rather than serving their own interests. Insofar as sustainability issues carry material financial risks, Trustees need to consider these issues as a core part of fiduciary duty.

UNEP FI and the PRI published a report on the changing landscape of fiduciary duty (PRI, 2019a). In that report it specifically noted the need for ESG issues to be considered as part of the investment process and identified the potential for Trustees to come under greater scrutiny in terms of their capacity, competency, and professionalism in this regard (Box 1).

Box 1: Modern Fiduciary Duty

Fiduciary duties (or equivalent obligations) exist to ensure that those who manage other people's money act in the interests of beneficiaries, rather than serving their own interests. The most important of these duties are:

- Loyalty – Fiduciaries should:
  - Act honestly and in good faith in the interests of their

beneficiaries or their clients.

- **Understand and incorporate into their decision making the sustainability preferences of beneficiaries and/or clients, whether or not these preferences are financially material.**
- Impartially balance the conflicting interests of different beneficiaries and clients.
- Avoid conflicts of interest.
- Not act for the benefit of themselves or third parties.

• Prudence – Fiduciaries should act with due care, skill and diligence, investing as an 'ordinary prudent person' would. This includes:
  - **Incorporating financially material ESG factors into their investment decision making, consistent with the timeframe of the obligation.**
  - Being an active owner, encouraging high standards of ESG performance in the companies or other entities in which they are invested.
  - Supporting the stability and resilience of the financial system.

Fiduciaries should disclose their investment approach to clients and/or beneficiaries including information on how preferences are incorporated into the scheme's investment strategy and the potential risks and benefits of doing so.

Source: PRI (2019a)

What the discussions on fiduciary duty are missing is a wider acknowledgement of the broader sense of purpose and social responsibility of the financial sector, that seeks to build a safer, more sustainable, and ethically sound system as part of how it functions (Lagarde, 2019). This goes beyond crafting a legal text or corporate statement that is imposed on people from the outside. It means stepping back and asking questions differently – whose needs am I serving? What are those needs? Is this the best way to serve those needs? Am I comfortable with what I am doing? Could I do it differently? In view of climate change and the planetary boundaries that we are testing, am I allocating capital to where it needs to go to best serve those needs?

Greenwashing

> *"Greenwashing distorts relevant information that a current or prospective investor might require in order to make informed investment decisions. It can erode investor confidence in the market for sustainability-related products and poses a threat to a fair and efficient financial system."*
> Armour (2021)

While there is positive momentum building amongst some financial institutions, there are also growing concerns of 'greenwashing' reverberating across the globe (Powell, 2022), as the momentum to support and align with sustainability goals has resulted in some exaggerated claims of activities and outcomes.

One of the high-profile exposés in the financial sector came from a former Group Sustainability Officer at German Asset Manager DWS and latterly whistleblower on the organization's sustainability claims. Fixler stated (cited in Eccles, 2023):

> *"It quickly became apparent to me that there was a big gap between their [DWS] public ESG claims and the reality of their ESG efforts. I tried hard to raise this internally...I explained that*

> *a number of their ESG statements in the Annual Report and other public releases were not only unsubstantiated but were seriously exaggerated, misleading, and just wrong…*
>
> *… they [DWS management] not only ignored me but actually made fun of the American strict regulatory compliance culture. Then it got ugly. They basically fired me and leaked a story to Bloomberg in an attempt to control the narrative."*

Despite denial by the DWS management of any untoward conduct, a German federal police raid ensued and the CEO Asoka Woehrmann was ousted, as well as a number of other senior executives (Fortune, 2022). *"I think that pretty much says it all"* noted Fixler (cited in Eccles, 2023).

This example is somewhat a special case in that it highlights the potential depths of the deceit that could emanate within organisations when they take up the sustainability mantle for the wrong reasons. Not all organisations have an individual with the knowledge, courage and fortitude to confront management if misleading statements or information is being put out into the public domain on sustainability achievements or actions. This is why financial regulators are stepping in to combat greenwashing (ECOFACT, n.d.).

Many of the antidotes to 'greenwashing' that are widely discussed and being adopted include tighter regulations, penalties, auditing and clearer definitions and classification of sustainability activities. Such measures are aimed at fostering greater alignment and consistency in sustainability practices and disclosures across organisations and jurisdictions, with greater visibility and potential penalties being the 'stick' that prevents organisations from publicly over-stating their achievements.

The problem of course is that even with enhanced reporting and auditing processes in place, it will be very difficult for regulators to keep up with the myriad of ways that organisations could find to present themselves in a favourable light. The definitions of what is 'green' or 'sustainable' is still evolving and varies across regions, with some jurisdictions being more stringent than others. This makes comparability and reporting quite challenging for global financial institutions, even when sustainability taxonomies exist. Many of the initiatives that organisations publicly commit to, such as the SDGs or Net Zero by 2050, are aspirational initially with a significant time lag before any signs of progress or outcomes need to be demonstrated.

Moreover, if the 'stick' to combat greenwashing is too heavy handed, it could have the perverse effect of slowing down progress and action, as there is a greater perceived risk around communication of sustainability activities that causes some organisations to quietly withdraw. This is emerging as the so-called 'green hushing' effect, where organisations are going quiet on sustainability issues (Corporate Governance Institute, n.d.), or even withdrawing from initiatives that they fear might put the spotlight too much on them (Wilkes, 2023).

Summary

The financial sector has a key role to play in shifting the global economy towards a more sustainable trajectory. A growing number of international financial institutions are collaborating to integrate ESG issues into decision-making processes, align with the SDGs, support a 'just and fair' Net Zero by 2050, reduce habitat and biodiversity loss, and engage in relevant policy debates to help achieve these goals. These actions are being encouraged and reinforced by a widespread shift in societal expectations, a rise in climate risk litigation cases, as well as increased scrutiny on sustainability issues (particularly climate change) by central banks and financial regulators. However, there is also increased scrutiny on the exaggerated claims made by some financial institutions with respect to sustainability, with growing concern about greenwashing. As some organisations back pedal on their sustainability messaging to avoid such scrutiny, we are now witnessing a wave of so-called 'green hushing'.

There is a fairly straightforward solution to break this negative cycle of sustainability claims, counter-claims, regulations, litigation cases, and inconsistencies in continuing to finance harmful activities. It is to look at the prevailing mindsets.

If we bring greater awareness and focus on the inner dimensions and workings of the people who work inside the financial sector - and those that are connected to and oversee the sector - then we can build an environment where the urge to take action comes not only from externally imposed drivers, but is also a reflection of our how we (individually and collectively) think about issues, how we process information and hence how we behave.

References

Armour, C. (2021). What is "greenwashing" and what are its potential threats? Armour, C. (2021). What is "greenwashing" and what are its potential threats? https://asic.gov.au/about-asic/news-centre/articles/what-is-greenwashing-and-what-are-its-potential-threats/.

ASFI. (2022). Analysis of international taxonomies and considerations for Australia Australian Sustainable Finance Institute Taxonomy Project. https://www.asfi.org.au/taxonomy.

Banque de France. (2019). NGFS publications. https://www.ngfs.net/en/liste-chronologique/ngfs-publications.

BloombergNEF. (2023). The Biodiversity Finance Factbook. A report published by BloombergNEF.

Eccles, R.G. (2023). 'A whistleblower's tale' As told by Desiree Fixler. Forbes. https://www.forbes.com/sites/bobeccles/2023/01/17/a-whistleblowers-tale-as-told-by-desiree-fixler/?sh=3b2f206164d1.

ECOFACT. (n.d.). Regulators are intensifying their scrutiny of greenwashing. https://www.ecofact.com/blog/regulators-are-intensifying-their-scrutiny-of-greenwashing/.

European Central Bank. (2009). Financial stability review. https://www.ecb.europa.eu/pub/pdf/fsr/art/ecb.fsrart200912en_05.pdf.

European Commission. (2022). Overview of sustainable finance. [online] finance.ec.europa.eu. https://finance.ec.europa.eu/sustainable-finance/overview-sustainable-finance_en.

Financial Standards Board. (2020). Stocktake of financial authorities' experience in including physical and transition climate risks as part of their financial stability monitoring. https://www.fsb.org/wp-content/uploads/P220720.pdf.

Force for Good. (n.d.). Sustainable finance, sustainable development goals. Available at: https://www.forcegood.org/finance-as-a-force-for-good.

Fortune. (2022). Deutsche Bank raided by authorities over ESG 'greenwashing' claims. https://fortune.com/2022/05/31/deutsche-bank-dws-esg-greenwashing-raid-evidence-seized-whistleblower-fixler/.

Friend, I. (1972). The economic consequences of the stock market. The American Economic Review, 62(1/2), 212–219. http://www.jstor.org/stable/182154574 Ibid 213.

Glasgow Financial Alliance for Net Zero. (2021). Call to action. https://www.gfanzero.com/press/call-to-action/.

Global Impact Investing Network. (n.d.). Impact investing trends: evidence of a growing industry. https://thegiin.org/research/publication/impact-investing-trends.

Global Reporting Initiative, the UN Global Compact and the World Business Council for Sustainable Development. (n.d.). SDG Compass: The Guide for Business Action on the SDGs. https://sdgcompass.org/.

IMF. (2019). The Financial Sector: Redefining a Broader Sense of Purpose. Available at: https://www.imf.org/en/News/Articles/2019/02/21/sp022819-md-the-financial-sector-redefining-a-broader-sense-of-purpose.

International Energy Agency. (2021). Net Zero by 2050: A Roadmap for the Global Energy Sector. https://www.iea.org/reports/net-zero-by-2050.

Intergovernmental Panel on Climate Change. (2023). AR6 Synthesis Report: Climate Change. https://www.ipcc.ch/report/sixth-assessment-report-cycle/.

Intergovernmental Panel on Climate Change. (2018). Global Warming of 1.5°C. An IPCC Special Report on the impacts of global warming of 1.5°C above pre-industrial levels and related global greenhouse gas emission pathways, in the context of strengthening the global response to the threat of climate change, sustainable development, and efforts to eradicate poverty.

Lagarde, C. (2019). The Financial Sector: Redefining a Broader Sense of Purpose, 32nd World Traders' Tacitus Lecture, United Kingdom.

London Business School. (n.d.). The finance industry: what's its purpose? London Business School. Available at: https://www.london.edu/think/the-purpose-of-the-finance-industry.

Network for Greening the Financial System. (2023). Annual Report. https://www.ngfs.net/en/annual-report-2022.

North, G., and Buckley, R.P. (2010). A fundamental re-examination of efficiency in capital markets in light of the global financial crisis. UNSW Law Journal, Vol.33(3):714-744.

OECD. (2021). De-risking institutional investment in green infrastructure: 2021 progress update. OECD Environment Policy Papers, No. 28, OECD Publishing, Paris, https://doi.org/10.1787/357c027e-en.

OECD. (2020). Developing Sustainable Finance Definitions and Taxonomies. Green Finance and Investment, OECD Publishing, Paris, https://doi.org/10.1787/134a2dbe-en.

Planet Tracker. (2022). Nature Dependent Exporters: What do they have in common? https://planet-tracker.org/wp-content/uploads/2022/10/NDE-report.pdf.

Powell, D. (2022). Wishing or washing? Green investment claims under spotlight. [online] The Sydney Morning Herald. Available at: https://www.smh.com.au/money/investing/wishing-or-washing-green-claims-under-spotlight-20220711-p5b0o8.html.

Principles for Responsible Investment. (2021). A legal framework for impact: Sustainability impact in investor decision-making. https://www.unpri.org/download?ac=13902.

Principles for Responsible Investment. (2020). Beyond ESG incorporation: how the SDGs can help investors shape outcomes in the world. ttps://www.unpri.org/pri-blog/beyond-esg-incorporation-how-the-sdgs-can-help-investors-shape-outcomes-in-the-world/5921.article.

Principles for Responsible Investment. (2019a). Fiduciary Duty in the 21st Century. https://www.unpri.org/download?ac=9792.

Principles for Responsible Investment. (2019b). Principles for Investors in Inclusive Finance (PIIF). https://www.unpri.org/investment-tools/thematic-and-impact-investing.

Principles for Responsible Investment. (n.d.) What is Responsible Investment? https://www.unpri.org/about/what-is-responsible-investment.

Principles for Responsible Investment. (n.d.). Investing with SDG outcomes: a five-part framework. https://www.unpri.org/sustainable-development-goals/investing-with-sdg-outcomes-a-five-part-framework/5895.article.

Sandel, M.J. (2013). The Moral Economy of Speculation: Gambling, Finance, and the Common Good. In Tanner Lectures on Human Values. University of Utah. Publisher's Version.

Statista Research Department. (2023). Assets of financial institutions worldwide 2002-2021. www.statista.com

Stracca, L. (2004). Behavioral finance and asset prices: Where do we stand?, Journal of Economic Psychology, 25, issue 3, p. 373-405, https://EconPapers.repec.org/RePEc:eee:joepsy:v:25:y:2004:i:3:p:373-405.

Task Force on Nature-related Financial Disclosures. (2023). The TNFD Nature-related Risk and Opportunity Management and Disclosure Framework: Beta v0.4 – Summary. https://tnfd.global/.

Task Force on Climate-related Financial Disclosures. (2022). TCFD Status Report: Task Force on Climate-related Financial Disclosures. https://www.fsb.org/2022/10/2022-tcfd-status-report-task-force-on-climate-related-financial-disclosures/.

Task Force on Climate-related Financial Disclosures. (2017). Final Report: Recommendations of the Task Force on Climate-related

Financial Disclosures. https://www.fsb-tcfd.org/publications/final-recommendations-report/.

The Corporate Governance Institute. (n.d.). What is green-hushing? https://www.thecorporategovernanceinstitute.com/insights/lexicon/what-is-green-hushing/.

United Nations Brundtland Commission (1987). Report of the World Commission on Environment and Development: Our Common Future. [online] p.16. Available at: http://www.un-documents.net/our-common-future.pdf.

United Nations Climate Change. (2022). Race to Zero Campaign: Halving emissions by 2030. https://unfccc.int/climate-action/race-to-zero-campaign.

United Nations Development Program. (2018). About the Sustainable Development Goals - United Nations Sustainable Development. [online] United Nations Sustainable Development. http://www.un.org/sustainabledevelopment/sustainable-development-goals/.

United Nations Development Program. (n.d.). United Nations Millennium Development Goals. https://www.un.org/millenniumgoals.

United Nations Environment Program. (2022). Emissions Gap Report (EGR) 2022: The Closing Window – Climate crisis calls for rapid transformation of societies. https://www.unep.org/resources/emissions-gap-report-2022.

United Nations Environment Program. (2017). The Financial System We Need: From Momentum to Transformation. UNEP Inquiry. http://unepinquiry.org/publication/the-financial-system-we-need-from- momentum-to-transformation/.

United Nations Environment Program. (n.d.). The Convention on Biological Diversity. https://www.cbd.int/convention/.

Waitzer, E. J., & Sarro, D. (2014). Fiduciary Society Unleashed: The Road Ahead for the Financial Sector. The Business Lawyer, 69(4), 1081–1116. http://www.jstor.org/stable/43666019.

Wilkes, T. (2023). Insurers' climate alliance loses nearly half its members after more quit. Reuters. https://www.reuters.com/business/insurers-climate-alliance-loses-nearly-half-its-members-after-more-quit-2023-05-30/.

World Bank Group. (2017). Financial Stability. World Bank. Retrieved from https://www.worldbank.org/en/publication/gfdr/gfdr-2016/background/financial-stability.

World Economic Forum. (2023). How the financial sector can spur the industrial economy's transition. https://www.weforum.org/agenda/2023/01/davos23-financial-sector-sustainable-development-stakeholder-capitalism/.

World Economic Forum. (2021). The Global Risks Report 2021: 16th Edition. Insight Report. WEF. http://www3.weforum.org/docs/WEF_The_Global_Risks_Report_2021.pdf.

World Meteorological Organization. (2023). Global temperatures set to reach new records in next five years. Global Annual to Decadal Climate Update. https://library.wmo.int/doc_num.php?explnum_id=11173.

2. Cultivating a sustainable mindset in finance

"Today's problems cannot be solved with the same level of thinking that created them."
Albert Einstein

"Organisations do not change. People change!"
Baggio et al (2019)

For the financial sector to integrate sustainability into its capital allocation decisions, it is essential that the mindset of individuals working inside the sector are in alignment with this goal. Our mindset influences how we think, which determines how we feel and how we behave – and how we behave collectively determines the outcome for the entire ecosystem. Without a sustainable mindset, there is a greater risk that even the best and well-intentioned sustainability policies, processes, products, and services will fall short of achieving their intended goal.

To embed sustainability into the finance sector's decision-making frameworks, we need to consider not only the external conditions that influence behaviour. We also need to consider the internal conditions or the 'mindset' of individuals inside the financial sector, and how that influences the integration of sustainability into their decision-making processes.

What is mindset, and why does it matter?

- Mindset refers to the way we think, and the way we view the world, what motivates us.
- A mindset is a mental attitude. It shapes our actions and our thoughts (Meier & Kropp, 2010).
- Mindset is the lens through which we view the world and our role/place in it, including the underlying assumptions, beliefs, and values that inform that lens (Kassel et al, 2016).
- Mindsets are a set of assumptions that help you distill complex worldviews into digestible information and then set expectations based on this input (Towery, 2023).
- Mindset matters as we may not be fully aware or able to articulate it, but it will reveal itself in our words and our actions.
- Mindsets can and do change over time as our brains and neural responses are adaptive, especially if we are willing to learn and grow (Ng, 2018).
- Mindsets influence how quickly and effectively we are willing to adapt our thinking in response to new industry developments, such as the rapid adoption of sustainability principles into corporate and investment frameworks.
- Many efforts to transform organisations have failed due to a lack of focus on understanding the mindsets that drive

behaviour. *"Unless you first identify the mindsets, both limiting and enabling your people, your transformation initiatives may be wasting resources, time and energy"* (Baggio et al, 2019:8).

- Mindset shifts are linked to the highest impact behaviours a person wants to change. Organisations that take the time to identify and shift deep-seated mindsets were 4x more likely to rate their change programs as successful (McKinsey, 2021).

Literature on mindsets

Dweck and Yaeger (2021) noted that mindset research originated from two lines of enquiry, namely learned helplessness or defeatism (Selignman & Maier, 1967) and attribution theory (Weiner & Kukla, 1970). Learned helplessness or defeatism showed that exposure to negative events can result in passive behaviour and a shutdown of sorts when people give up in the face of difficult situations. In the context of climate change, we can see that if the message is too negative and alarming, it could have the perverse effect of closing people down and turning away from climate action, as they become de-motivated and feel defeated by the enormity of the challenge.

Attribution theory showed the importance of people's perceptions and beliefs in shaping their motivations to act in a certain way. In the case of Dweck's research, this focused on a student's belief about their own intelligence, and how that impacted on their performance at school and later in life. In the context of climate change action, a person's perceptions and beliefs about climate change will influence how motivated they are to act.

These two foundations of knowledge have provided the platform for further mindset research over the past three decades, which extended this line of enquiry to examine how people's perceptions influence their motivation, and how that could be changed to alter behaviour. The mindset research led by Dweck (1975) and applied to the education sector, studied how mindsets influence student performance and resilience.

Businesses and organisations have also applied the mindset research in relation to the motivation and performance of employees (McKinsey, 2021). Other related fields of research have emerged, for example, neuroscientists have studied the connection between mindsets and neuroplasticity and the brain's neural networks, providing new perspectives on how mindsets are related to how brains change (Ng, 2018). The research has also been extended and applied to consider how to build a more sustainable world, led by Rimanoczy (2010, 2020) in the development of the sustainability mindset principles to support a better world.

Fixed and growth mindset characteristics

Dweck's work combines developmental psychology, social psychology, and personality psychology to research the education sector by focusing on the mindsets of students and what enables or inhibits their learning abilities. The framework resulted in a growth / fixed mindset schematic which has gained widespread adoption and utilisation in the education sector and other settings, including in the business world. The distinction between the fixed and growth mindset as defined by Dweck (2017) is a now widely cited and utilised framework in the academic and business settings. Figure 5 reproduces the fixed and growth mindset characteristics as set out by Dweck (2017).

Figure 5. Dweck, Mindset: changing the way you think to fulfil your potential

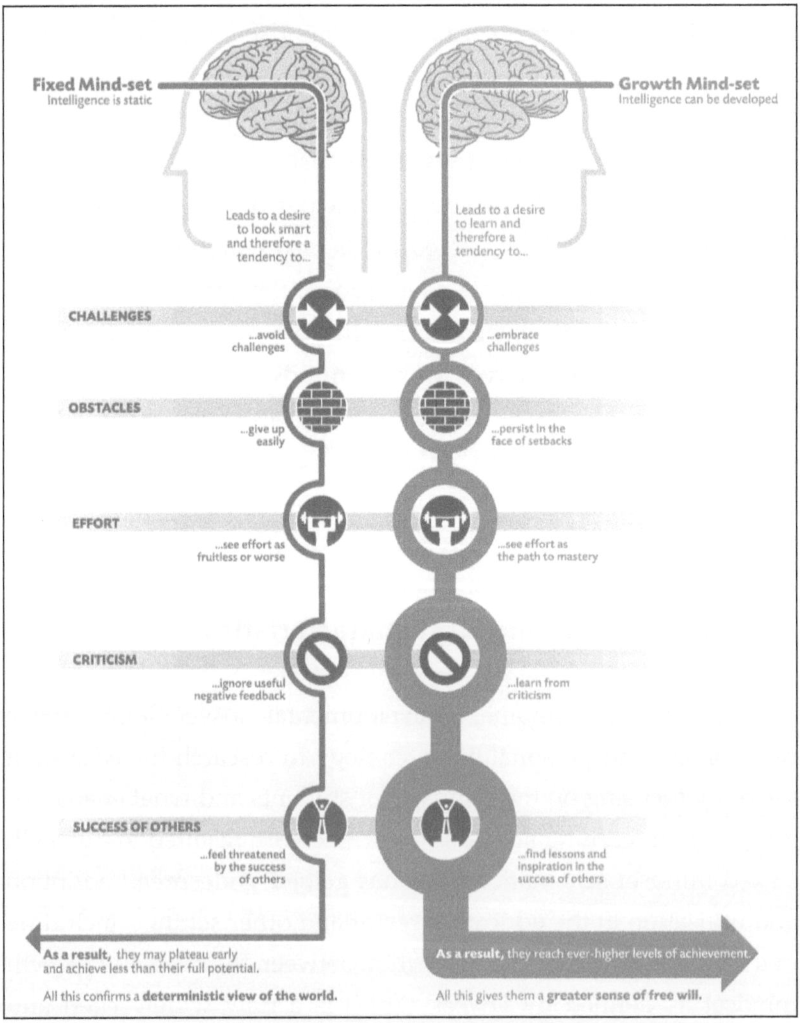

Source: Dweck, 2017:263

The characteristics of a growth or fixed mindset are further explained by Dweck (2012) as follows:

- Intelligence
  - A growth mindset sees intelligence as something that can be developed.
  - A fixed mindset sees intelligence as a fixed and static asset.

- Mistakes
  - A growth mindset embraces flaws and mistakes as an opportunity to improve.
  - A fixed mindset hides flaws and mistakes.

- Setbacks
  - A growth mindset accepts setbacks as part of the learning process.
  - A fixed mindset is ashamed of failure and unmotivated to achieve set goals.

- Feedback
  - A growth mindset welcomes feedback from others as an opportunity to grow.
  - A fixed mindset views feedback as personal criticism.

- Challenges
  - A growth mindset freely embraces challenges and risks probable failure.
  - A fixed mindset avoids challenges to avoid the possibility of failure.
- Success of others

 - A growth mindset sees other people's success as inspiration.
 - A fixed mindset sees other people's success as a threat to his success.

- Resolve
  - A growth mindset doesn't give up easily.
  - A fixed mindset gives up easily even at the slightest challenge.

The growth mindset is represented in the literature as being the more favorable mindset in different contexts, as it predisposes individuals to learn, aspire, be passionate and resilient, as Dweck (2017:7) noted:

> *"Why waste time proving over and over how great you are, when you could be getting better? Why hide deficiencies instead of overcoming them? Why look for friends or partners who will just shore up your self-esteem instead of ones who will always challenge you to grow? And why seek out the tried and true, instead of experiences that will stretch you?*
>
> *The passion for stretching yourself and sticking to it, even (or especially) when it's not going well, is the hallmark of the growth mindset. This is the mindset that allows people to thrive during some of the most challenging times in their lives."*

Dweck argued that a growth mindset can help people to be more adaptable and responsive to the changing demands and complexities of life. Many business schools and consultancies have also embraced the notion of a growth mindset and its appeal for 'business success'. For example, Wolfe (2022) set out five business benefits of a growth mindset to be:

1. Become a lifelong learner
2. Embrace challenges
3. Deal with setbacks
4. Become a better leader
5. Find meaning in your work

It is interesting to observe that most of these benefits are expressed in terms of the benefits to the business and the 'self' and not beyond that, although 'finding meaning in your work' invites a wider sense of purpose beyond the self. In contrast, a fixed mindset is represented as being negative, characterizing someone who gives up on life or shirks away from challenges:

> *"A fixed-minded person usually avoids challenges in life, gives up easily, and becomes intimidated or threatened by the success of other people. This is in part because a fixed mindset doesn't see intelligence and talent as something you develop—it's something you "are".*
>
> *Fixed mindsets can lead to negative thinking. For instance, a person with a fixed mindset might fail at a task and believe it's because they aren't smart enough to do it. Whereas a growth mindset person might fail at the same task and believe it's because they need to spend more time practicing."*
> Smith (2020:2)

The dominant narrative that prevails is therefore one in which the growth mindset is preferable to a fixed mindset, primarily because it will be of benefit to the 'self' and will help people to thrive in their life and their chosen profession.

This means that executives of multinational oil companies could have a growth mindset and be very adept at maximizing the business opportunities for profit and personal financial rewards. If such executives are rewarded for increasing extraction and refinery activities, and their personal values are not in conflict with such activities, then they are likely to steer the business in that direction. Consequently, their actions would contribute to increasing Co2 emissions and accelerating climate change outcomes, rather than reducing emissions and enabling a net zero by 2050 outcome.

As Watts (2021) observed:

> *"Executives have personal ownership of tens or hundreds of thousands of shares, which creates an unacknowledged personal desire to explore, extract and sell fossil fuels. That carbon mindset needs to be revised by realigning compensation towards success in lowering absolute emissions."*

This is just one example to illustrate why having a growth mindset will be preferable to a fixed mindset, but not sufficient to address the sustainability challenges of our time. Due to misaligned business and personal incentives, some executives are inadvertently encouraged to continue to 'grow' the extraction and utilization of fossil fuels, rather than innovate to shift to low carbon alternatives. If an executive's personal motivation to act on climate change was sufficiently strong, they could resist this temptation and invest more time and effort on seeking lower carbon alternatives to fossil fuels. But it would take more than just a 'growth' mindset to make that change.

From a sustainability perspective, it is not clear that a growth mindset will be sufficient to achieve outcomes such as closing the climate financing gap, attainment of the SDGs, Net Zero emissions, alleviate poverty, social justice or reduce biodiversity loss. While a growth mindset will create the *potential* for individuals to embrace change and challenges and to be persistent in the face of setbacks (personal qualities that will be beneficial to sustainability pursuits), it will be a person's passion, their values and motivations that will ultimately determine their actions and whether they contribute to solving the sustainability challenges of our time.

Another example of how leaders of an organization with a growth mindset can produce not only environmental damage but also social harm is the expansion of Rio Tinto's iron ore mining activities that resulted in the destruction of an ancient indigenous heritage site, the Juukan Gorge in Western Australia. In the immediate aftermath of the destruction of the site, the then CEO Chris Salisbury defended the action by pointing out that the project was legal as it had government approval and the indigenous community had been consulted but that *"Clearly, there was a misunderstanding"* (Wahlquist, 2020).

There was little in the way of personal regret expressed by the then CEO. According to media reports at the time (Wahlquist, 2020) the project appears to have been driven by a growth mindset that pursued the financial benefits of expanding iron ore mining activities in the Pilbara region. However, the public backlash in the aftermath of the destruction led not only to the CEO resigning, but also a holistic rethink of the values of Rio Tinto to change how the company does business. The incumbent CEO stated in 2022:

"In the two years since the tragic destruction of the rock shelters

> *at Juukan Gorge, on the land of the Puutu Kunti Kurrama and Pinikura people in Western Australia, we have been changing the way we work in every part of our business. While we have made progress, we know it will take time to transform our culture and regain trust. But, together with the Indigenous peoples of the lands on which we operate, we are committed to ensuring cultural heritage is respected, valued and conserved for future generations."*
> Jakob Stausholm, Chief Executive, https://www.riotinto.com/en/news/inquiry-into-juukan-gorge

These examples show that leaders can set the tone and direction of an organization, and that a growth mindset will not be sufficient to achieve sustainable outcomes. In the case of Rio Tinto, a new CEO was appointed to review and reinvigorate the company's approach to respect indigenous rights at a deeper, more fundamental level than they had done in the past. Time will tell if such claims are genuine and result in real change in approaches to project management and strategic planning.

In summary, sustainability needs to be part of an individual's personal beliefs and motivations, otherwise the effort to address challenges and adapt to the changing business landscape with a growth mindset could result in outcomes that contribute to further degradation of the environment and harm to local communities and culture.

> It will be harder (but not impossible) for people with a fixed mindset to want to adapt to an enlarged sense of purpose that embeds sustainability at its core. People with a growth mindset will be more open to change and willing to adapt, although they may not have aligned their personal beliefs and

motivations with such a pursuit, or they may be unsure about what it means in practice and still have some way to go before that goal can be realised.

Sustainability mindset characteristics

This brings us to the emerging body of research on sustainability mindsets, led by Rimanoczy, convener of the UN PRME Working Group on the Sustainability Mindset.[1] Rimanoczy studied sustainability leaders in the corporate sector and observed that their actions related to a combination of their knowledge, how they thought about sustainability issues, their values and sense of purpose (2010). Rimanoczy also observed that the laudable goals underpinning the SDGs and the pursuit of sustainability were predominantly focused on solutions related to the external, or "visible" parts of sustainability – such as knowledge and information, regulations, policies, benchmarks, and best practice standards. In contrast, there was little focus on the internal or "hidden" parts of sustainability (our beliefs, how we think, how we make sense of the world), although the prevailing research on mindsets showed how important these internal processes are for understanding our motivations and behaviour.

This led Rimanoczy to a deep enquiry into the mindsets of some corporate managers who had demonstrated leadership on sustainability issues. The goal of the research was to better understand the characteristics of how these leaders think, what motivates them, how they are willing to stand out from the crowd and utilize their power and influence in ways that benefit others and the environment. This also made them feel good and the businesses themselves thrived, a win-win for the planet and the bottom line. The research methods were primarily qualitative in nature, garnering stories and sharing experiences from these leaders, which culminated in the development of the sustainability mindset characteristics through the application of grounded theory.

The sustainability mindset was defined by Kassel, Rimanoczy and Mitchell (2016) as:

> *"A way of thinking and being that results from a broad understanding of the ecosystem's manifestations, from social sensitivity, as well as an introspective focus on one's personal values and higher self, and finds its expression in actions for the greater good of the whole."*

The sustainability mindset therefore relates not only to a person's knowledge and understanding about the ecosystem, but also how information is processed and the meaning that is given to this knowledge, that is, a person's values and beliefs. In building this understanding, the sustainability principles invite a shift in individual and collective behaviours through a process of enquiry and questioning.

> The sustainability mindset principles are intended to accelerate action on sustainability issues, to solve the challenges that we face at the individual and collective level. They are intended to guide the internal inquiry process, not to prescribe a list of specific actions and outcomes for every imaginable context or situation, which would not only be an impossible task but also one that would not encourage a process of self-enquiry.

Rimanoczy (2020) set out four content areas and 12 principles that comprise a sustainable mindset as summarised in Figure 6.

Figure 6. The Sustainability Mindset Principles

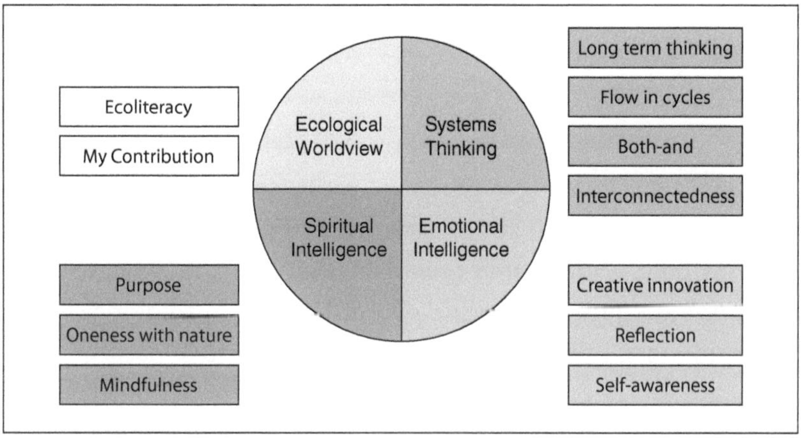

Source: Rimanoczy (2021:21)

Ecological worldview

The ecological worldview refers to our understanding of the state of the planet and how we feel about it. It is comprised of two underlying principles, namely Ecoliteracy and My contribution:

1. Ecoliteracy - Understanding the state of the planet to be more fully aware of the challenges, the complexity and interlinkages, and to explore what it means to us. It goes beyond an understanding of the scientific evidence and encourages a deeper understanding of interconnections, personal engagement and emotional reaction.

2. My contribution – Identify the ways in which we are

unintentionally contributing to the problems, so that we are in a better position to do something about them. It increases awareness and looks to build the habit of exploring unintentional contribution in our thoughts and actions.

Systems perspective

The systems perspective focuses on processing information using a systemic lens, looking at the flows, processes and feedback loops and systems nested in larger systems, and how they all integrate into a whole. Within this school of thought, the sustainability mindset highlighted the principles of Long-term thinking, Both+ and thinking, Cyclical flow and Interconnectedness.

3. Long-term thinking – Every action has consequences that are not immediately visible. Considering the long term when analysing situations and making decisions has a positive impact on global sustainability. It aims to build the habit of considering long-term impacts.

4. Both+ and thinking – Allows us to understand paradoxes and calls for creative solutions that are inclusive of all stakeholders. To see the either/or factor at play and intentionally promote both+ and thinking.

5. Flow in cycles – Everything flows in cycles of birth, growth, death and rebirth. Many aspects of human unsustainability of the planet are a result of the misconceptions that we are not governed by this law of Nature. The aim is to develop the cognitive habit of seeing the larger cycles.

6. Interconnectedness – When we see interconnectedness between all living organisms and species, we understand the importance of diversity, and our decisions and actions become more inclusive, which contributes to the sustainability of the whole.

Emotional intelligence

Emotional intelligence refers to introspective practices to increase self-awareness and explore personal values. It includes the principles of Creative innovation, Reflection and Self-awareness.

7. Creative innovation – Resilience is based on constant creativity, innovation and experimentation. We look to enhance our personal potential for creative imagination, to experiment with new ways of doing things and solving problems.

8. Reflection – Reflective practices help to pause and ponder the situation and its implications before jumping into our automatic response and behaviour. Explore our assumptions and the paradigm that we work within and consider alternative perspectives.

9. Self-awareness – Explore our personal values, beliefs, assumptions and motivations to gain greater control over our actions, and to see alternative behaviours. Uncover and question the tacit assumptions that guide our behaviours.

Spiritual intelligence

The spiritual intelligence refers to our innate wisdom on questions of purpose, transcendence and oneness. It includes principles of Purpose, Oneness with nature and Mindfulness.

10. Purpose – Defining our purpose provides an unconscious compass, and when it is grounded in values of our higher self, we actively shape a better world. Identify what we feel passionate about that can make a difference for the greater good.

11. Oneness with nature – Understanding that we are one with Nature can shape behaviours, leading to a more harmonious relationship with each other and all beings.

12. Mindfulness – Being fully present, experiencing connectedness with all that is. Mindfulness enhances awareness and compassion and predisposes to social and environmental actions.

In summary, the 12 sustainable mindset principles provide the scaffolding for how we can think about sustainability through a lens that invites self-examination and exploration, to look closer at our inner workings and see if there is a different way to respond to the complexities that the sustainability challenge presents. As Rimanoczy (2021) noted, the sustainable mindset principles are intended to be general in nature, allowing the application and emphasis of the principles to be utilised, as appropriate, in different contexts. As Rimanoczy (2021:4) noted:

> *"There is no one way to develop a mindset for sustainability.... The vision was to have a few principles, clear and easily*

> *understandable statements, which could guide educators around the world to find ways to embed sustainable mindset goals... Yes, a mindset shift is urgent, but HOW can we do that?"*

We will now apply this scaffolding to examine the specific context of the financial sector, to see how a widespread mindset shift can emerge. We will start by exploring some of the literature that is relevant to developing the sustainability mindset in the context of the financial sector, before moving on to look at a proposed framework that brings these insights together.

Additional literature relevant to cultivating a sustainability mindset in finance

As we consider how the sustainability mindset principles could be applied to the finance sector, it is helpful to review the additional literature and evidence that is relevant in the context of the financial sector. The literature has been distilled into three areas (Figure 7), namely:

1. Emotion – how we feel;
2. Cognition – how we think; and
3. Behaviours – how we behave.

Figure 7.

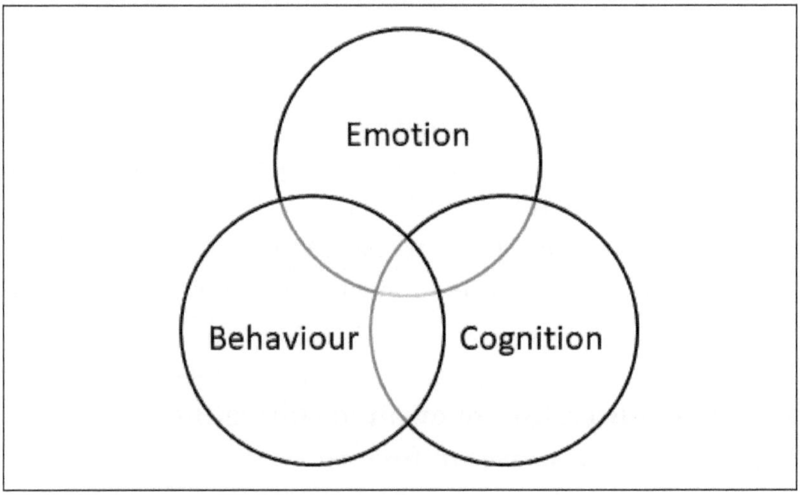

These three areas are interdependent; that is, if we behave a certain way it will trigger particular emotions; if we think a certain way, it will instigate certain behaviours and emotions; if we feel a certain way, it will lead to certain thoughts and behaviours. In other words, this is not a linear, deterministic process where we can predict that a) will lead to b). It is a dynamic and recursive framework, where there is common ground and shared drivers of our emotional, cognitive and behavioural conditions, but at the same time these will be unique to everyone.

By considering the literature and evidence related to each of these areas for the financial sector, we can better understand the internal barriers to sustainability action for this sector, and therefore move closer to revealing possible actions that will help to cultivate a sustainable mindset shift.

Emotion – how we feel

> *"In order to have anything like a complete theory of human rationality, we have to understand what role emotion plays in it" (Simon, 1982:29)*

In neoclassical economics, emotion is a subject that is usually treated as an outlier to rational decision-making, as a barrier to the homo-economicus construct (Dixon and Wilson, 2013). As we will see from the literature and evidence, emotion can indeed deviate markedly from the notion of rationality, but this doesn't necessarily reflect a 'bias' that needs to be redressed, it is rather illustrative of the complexity of the human condition and what makes us function. It is not a question of whether emotions influence decision-making (Damasio, 1994) but rather to acknowledge that emotions are an inseparable component of our decisions and choices.

Some of the research on emotion in the context of investors has discovered that emotion can in fact be a dominant driver behind short termism and other cognitive patterns of behaviour. Feeling or emotion-based automatic judgements have also been found to explain attribution errors and problems of self-control, such as fear of risky choices (Hirshleifer, 2001).

Our emotional brain is a key part of building an understanding as to why we are pulled towards the short term. People have difficulty imagining the future, even though our logical brain clearly sees the future consequences of our current actions. For example, our emotional brain wants to push our credit card to its limit, or smoke cigarettes, whereas our logical brain knows we should save for retirement and quit smoking. To understand why we feel internally conflicted and how this could be managed, it therefore helps to know how the emotional and abstract reasoning parts of the brain talk to each other (Schultz, 2004).

Studies have explored the possibility of re-biasing behaviour by "intelligently" working on emotions to improve the quality of decisions (Bouzguenda, 2018). The cultivation of emotional intelligence in the financial sector means that we can take action to harness the emotions that support positive behaviours and outcomes, and reduce those that are harmful. While there is no magic recipe for achieving emotional intelligence in the financial sector, Bouzguenda (2018) suggested that education and training on emotional intelligence could help to improve decision-making processes and change how people react to situations on a day-to-day basis. This means including emotional intelligence training in the context of schools, colleges, academic and industry education as well as integration into organisational training programs. Organisations could also include emotional intelligence in human resource policies and practices, as well as hiring techniques, such that a culture evolves whereby "*emotional intelligence becomes not only a value but also a factor of performance on-the job.*" (Bouzguenda: 2018:19).

In the context of sustainability within the financial sector, emotion can at times undermine our sustainability actions (fear of change can lead to resistance, for example). It can also be a powerful motivator for action and central to the sustainable mindset change process if it is recognised and harnessed in the right way. This process starts with cultivating emotional intelligence which includes building increased self-awareness, self-regulation, motivation, empathy, and social skills (Goleman, 1995), to help people and organisations adapt and change.

One of the ways that the investment community has approached their emotional connection to sustainability is to consider definitions around purpose and beliefs. These considerations are often put into the governance category in the investment context, which typically refers to the people and structures in place to ensure there is effective oversight and management of the investment processes. For example, in the context of the TCFD recommendations specific to climate change, governance was one of the four pillars of the recommendations (TCFD, 2017). The recommended actions include describing the board's oversight of climate-related risks and opportunities and describing management's role in assessing and managing climate-related risks and opportunities. Nowhere in the text is there reference to how people think, what attitudes they bring to the issues, how their emotions, feelings and assumptions might be influencing how they make decisions. This is quite typical of other guidance on investment actions specific to governance and is not a criticism specific to the TCFD.

Consequently, while reference to governance is a valuable and much needed addition to the investment frameworks as they at least acknowledge that there are people involved in the process, they still gloss over the inner dimensions of the human condition. By remaining on the outer edge of enquiry into how investor's feel about sustainability issues and how their emotions influence their behaviour, we are also overlooking how we can genuinely shift to a system that incorporates sustainability into its core.

Embracing a broader sense of purpose

On the connection to purpose, much of the debate within the financial sector resides in the definition and interpretation of fiduciary duty. Many international legal experts have studied the laws in their regions and generally agree (with some variation) that the fiduciary duty of a financial institution is to act in the best interest of their stakeholders, which has been interpreted to mean best financial interest (PRI, 2019). Additional text has been added to reference ESG and sustainability issues as being financially material considerations, therefore an integral part of these duties.

Legal cases have proliferated to challenge investors who have failed to consider sustainability as part of their purpose, with no cases (at the time of writing) that have pursued an institution because they acted on sustainability.[2] That means that from a purely legal perspective, the risk of inaction on sustainability is higher than the risk of action. Organisations do, however, need to demonstrate that they are integrating sustainability and ESG issues in a genuine way, to avoid accusations of greenwashing and the potential legal ramifications of that. But let's be clear, legal action against greenwashing poses a risk only to organisations that say they are doing something when they are not doing it. So, there is only a risk if there is an element of deception or exaggeration. In all cases the onus will be on investors to have a clear process and rationale in place for why they are acting on sustainability, how they are acting and what they hope to achieve. Honesty and clarity are principles that apply to the incorporation of any issue that impact on investment decisions and outcomes, sustainability should not be considered a unique or additional source of risk from that perspective if it is embedded into processes in a genuine way.

What the discussions on fiduciary duty are missing is a wider acknowledgement of the emotional connection to a sense of purpose that warrants attention. As we will see when we turn to examine short-termism, the brain's urge to make short term decisions is dominated by an emotional drive to do so, as it seeks short term reward and feedback. The logical inference is therefore not to deny that emotion exists or needs to be stamped out, but to consider how investors can harness their emotions to personally feel connected to a broader sense of purpose that guides their day-to-day behaviour.

This goes beyond crafting a legal text or corporate statement that is imposed on people from the outside. It means stepping back and asking questions differently – whose needs am I serving? What are those needs? Is this the best way to serve those needs? Am I comfortable with what I am doing? Could I do it differently? Am I allocating capital to where it needs to go to best serve those needs? How would I explain this decision to someone if they asked how it fitted with our sustainability goals?

As the Institute of Chartered Accountants in England and Wales (ICAEW, 2018) observed in the aftermath of the global financial crisis, the financial sector needs to develop a clear understanding and belief in purpose. This will provide people and organisations with the context and resilience to make difficult decisions and help to cement good culture and conduct. ICAEW noted that purpose needs to be easily understood by everyone, so that it can provide a coherent approach to implement change and new initiatives, developments and practices.

"Believing in the "why" behind a change can inspire people to

> *change their behaviour. In practice, however, we find that many transformation leaders falsely assume that the "why" is clear to the broader organization and consequently fail to spend enough time communicating the rationale behind change efforts."*
> Basford and Schaninger (2016:8)

According to Sinek (2019), most organisations and people start with the 'what' and think about more functional aspects of what they do. They are also able to articulate 'how' they do what they do, listing goods/services that they provide and tools that they use. However, genuine behaviours that can be sustained over time need to start with the 'why' a person is doing what they are doing, what it personally means to them. This purpose is more than making money for a client or end beneficiary, that is an outcome. The 'why' is your purpose, what you believe in, it will run through everything you do and provide the common thread to all your decisions, it is part of your mindset.

The former director of the IMF and current President of the European Central Bank, Lagarde (2019) stated that a broader sense of purpose was needed for the financial sector:

> *"I believe that we can build a better financial sector — one that is safer, more sustainable, and ethically sound. A financial industry with a broader sense of purpose.*
>
> *This goal is not just morally just; it is economically right. Why? Because a better financial sector is more important than ever to help deliver on what our 21st century so badly needs: higher employment, greener growth, and good living standards for all.*
>
> *The key to achieving this goal is to reshape finance into something that is more aligned with societal values and more connected to*

> *the interests of all stakeholders: from customers, to workers, to shareholders, to local communities and future generations."* (Lagarde, 2019)

Lagarde also observed that for finance to become safer and more trustworthy, it needs to harness innovation, better regulation, and a broader sense of responsibility. She spoke about the importance of values and ethics and moral conduct, where each person working in finance needs to feel a broader sense of purpose that they are connected to and feel inspired to be creative and innovative to overcome obstacles and help achieve that reality.

While this vision of a financial industry with a broader sense of purpose – that seeks to build a safer, more sustainable, and ethically sound system as part of how it functions – might appear to be a long way from where we today, we will also see that with some minor adjustments to our prevailing mindsets, this vision could indeed become a reality. When hearts and minds are in alignment, then anything is possible. We already have the basis of widespread awareness of the challenges and opportunities that face us across the finance sector, the motivation to act is clear and present as we saw in Chapter 2 with the plethora of investment statements, goals, and certain actions. All it takes from here is to focus on those remaining gaps, the ones that are stickier and less examined than others, the gaps that emanate not from the external environment, but from how we think.

Realisation and alignment of beliefs

Defining the investment beliefs is another important component of developing a solid foundation for the development and implementation of a sustainability policy and program of work, for any financial institution. The Thinking Ahead Institute (2017) noted:

> *"The complexity of implementing a strategy for sustainability is considerable. Given the impossibility of reducing market behaviour and portfolio uncertainty to a series of equations, a system of beliefs is needed as the foundation of an accountable, methodical investment process."*

This perspective is generally accepted and endorsed by financial regulators, industry bodies and investor groups across different jurisdictions (Norton Rose Fulbright, 2022). For example, the PRI (2016) noted that investment beliefs set the direction for investment policy, practice, and organisational culture. Beliefs can not only help define how value will be created in the context of uncertainty, but they also help to guide capital allocation decisions.

Most financial institutions have gone through a process of defining their investment beliefs, with invariably some integration of sustainability and climate change issues as part of this process. Some financial institutions might have a stand-alone set of sustainability beliefs that go into considerable detail on specific ESG issues (EAPF, n.d.), while others will stay at a higher, principle-based level (BCI, n.d.). In almost all cases, the main challenge for organisations is to ensure that the beliefs are more than just words written on paper, and they are internalised by the individuals who make the day-to-day investment decisions.

While there is some variation in terms of the way that the industry goes about defining their beliefs and how that relates to sustainability issues, typically a board or committee will be guided (often by external advisors) to discuss and debate a range of sustainability issues. The result will normally set out the issues that the individuals inside the organisation (and their stakeholders) are most concerned about, the strength of their beliefs, and what that means in terms of the investment decision-making process (Thinking Ahead Institute, 2017).

The motivation or discussion as to 'why' a certain belief is important or has been adopted also links back to the broader sense of purpose that we discussed. Often the most contentious points will be the extent to which people see the pursuit of sustainability as being in alignment with (and necessary to) achieving strong financial outcomes, versus those that are less sure and envisage a trade-off of some kind. This tends to give rise to a case-by-case approach, or the preference towards implementation through actions that are not specific to capital allocation decisions but might still exert some influence over the outcomes (such as voting and engagement with investee companies, giving rise to engagement initiatives such as the CA100+).[3]

What is often missing from these actions and discussions is an explicit focus on the link between capital allocation decisions and creating positive real-world outcomes, whereby investors shift their thinking from being a responder to the external conditions that prevail, to one that is an enabler of a more sustainable future through their decisions. A lower level of conviction or weaker beliefs might stop short of making these connections, with some relegating this to the narrower remit of impact investing, rather than mainstream investing. It is crucial that boards, investment committees and everyone involved in this process spend time exploring how people feel about these arbitrary lines in the sand, as they are often based on assumptions that have not been challenged or deeply explored.

More fundamental questions might arise as part of this process such as: Do we believe that a more secure, safe, and prosperous world will be beneficial for our stakeholders and the people whose needs we are serving? Do we believe that we can help to create that world through our capital allocation decisions? Where is capital most needed to provide a secure, safe and prosperous world now and into the future? How can we accelerate our allocation to capital to these areas with the urgency that is required?

Cognition – how we think

In turning to how we think (our cognition), Kahneman (2011) provides an overarching framework that puts the rationality theory favoured by Plato, Aristotle, and the Enlightenment in a different light, by suggesting that humans are a product of our evolutionary environment and in many ways ill-equipped to deal with a rational, science-based, logical world. This means that we are all (investors included) at risk of repeating the same cognitive errors and biases, easily manipulated, and riven by sometimes irrational beliefs and fears. These tendencies have been classified by Kahneman (2011) in terms of fast and slow thinking responses, where fast thinking (referred to as System 1 thinking) refers to our automatic responses and decisions that are made quickly and with little effort. Slow thinking (System 2 thinking) allocates attention to the effortful mental activities that demand it, including complex computations. Kahneman argued that the notion of rationality would have us believe that System 2 thinking is prolific and dominant, although the evidence suggests that automatic thinking

with least effort is most common, tapping into Systems 2 thinking to confirm our automatic response or judgement.
This is an important body of work in the context of the finance sector, as it goes to the heart of how capital can be misallocated at the global level. Some of the identified psychological effects that can lead to inefficient allocation of capital include heuristic simplification, self-deception, narrow framing (Hirshleifer, 2001) and lack of systems thinking (Meadows, 2008). Daniel et al (2002) highlights how heuristic simplification might help to explain many investor biases such as availability effects (heavy focus on information that stands out), framing effects (where the description of a situation affects judgement), money illusion (where nominal prices affect perceptions) and status quo (where relied upon frameworks are not critically questioned). In addition, self-deception can explain overconfidence, biased self- attribution, confirmatory bias (interpret information in a way that is consistent with one's pre-existing beliefs) and anchoring to existing beliefs.

Two of the areas that warrant closer attention in relation to how we think and the ability of the financial sector to support and enable the shift to a sustainable financial system are systems thinking and long-term horizon. As we will see from the literature and evidence, narrow reductionist thinking tends to dominate how many investors make decisions, which can reduce their ability to see the connections and interrelationships at the system wide level. Reductionist thinking has emerged as the dominant and preferred mindset from a body of knowledge and learning since the industrial revolution to increase efficiency, but as we will see, it can be unlearned with some focus and effort to see the world in terms of interconnecting systems.

The second area of literature we will explore is the prevalence of short termism in the financial sector. This has been a well-documented and debated phenomena both in the academic and industry context, but to date there has been no real breakthrough or change to our myopic tendencies. We will explore why that is, if it can be overcome and some possible actions that could be taken.

Developing systems thinking

Aristotle observed that the whole is more important than the sum of its parts[4], which has been interpreted to mean that a system must be understood as a whole and cannot be comprehended by examining its individual parts in isolation from each other. That is the essence of what systems thinking means.

What we have seen over the past 400 years is an increasing tendency for people to segment their knowledge and understanding into smaller pieces and start to lose sight of the interconnections and relationships between these pieces. Ackoff (2004) explained that we have mistakenly come to view analysis and thinking as being synonymous. Analysis is, however, only one method of perceiving the world around us. Ackoff described what he coined synthetic thinking, where we try to explain the behaviour of the system and why the parts do what they do, compared to analytical thinking which tries to explain what the parts do and how they work. Ackoff (2004:4) noted that:

> *"Systemic thinking is holistic versus reductionistic thinking, synthetic versus analytic."*

As Atwater et al (2008) explained in the context of learning how to cultivate systems thinking, analytical thinking involves breaking down a system into smaller parts and examining them in isolation. Once the parts are understood, the analyst attempts to explain the behaviour of the whole based on the behaviour of the parts. In contrast, synthetic thinking attempts to *"understand the larger context that the system operates within"* (Atwater et al, 2008:12) to explain the behaviour of the system as a whole (Richmond, 2000). In other words, *"analytical thinking explains what the parts do and how they work while synthetic thinking explains why the parts do what they do"* (Atwater et al, 2008:12). Additional insights are offered by Meadows (2008:11) who defines a system as:

> *"…an interconnected set of elements that is coherently organized in a way that achieves something… A system must consist of three kinds of things: elements, interconnections and a function or purpose".*

In the context of the finance sector, the elements might be characterised as the traditional financial metrics that are utilised to evaluate the future value of a company or asset, whereas the interconnections are the linkages between the value of a company or asset and other conditions that stretch beyond these metrics (the macroeconomic, policy, political, social, and environmental context). The function or purpose as part of this framework links the systems thinking to how investors define their purpose, and the extent to which this is an enlarged sense of purpose that incorporates wider social and environmental responsibilities.

There is growing recognition from within some of the thought leaders of the financial sector on the benefits of systems thinking for the financial sector, although this is not yet the accepted wisdom of the mainstream investment community. As the Thinking Ahead Institute argued in its paper on system thinking and investment (2017:13):

> *"To better achieve their objectives in a complex adaptive system, participants need to utilise a multi-disciplinary approach to understanding, and managing, the system."*

We can see how important systems thinking is for the financial sector when we observe what happens at the system wide level when investors focus only on their individual part of the system and fail to see the whole or consider their wider responsibilities. The global financial crisis is an obvious example of such an event. At the system wide level, the continued financing of fossil fuel extraction activities in the face of catastrophic climate risks is another example, where the linkage between financing decisions and climate impacts is either not considered, not understood, not considered a priority, or not considered the best way to exert influence. It is such situations where we also see the liveliest debate within the finance sector, with some arguing that continued financing of fossil fuel activities while supporting net zero by 2050 goals is incompatible, whereas others justify this as a question of what lever to utilise and prefer to exercise their influence through engagement, whilst continuing to finance fossil fuel companies (Leaton, 2014).

A systems thinking approach would consider not only the individual parts (i.e., I am playing my part by engaging and asking fossil fuel companies to do better), but would consider the feedback loops and potential future consequences for the system as a whole (i.e., the increased risk of catastrophic climate outcomes due to continued expansion in fossil fuel extraction). An investor with this mindset would be very forceful in their engagement activities and clear in their expectations of what changes they want to see from fossil fuel companies by specific timelines and be prepared to withdraw their financing of such activities if such efforts are not achieving the desired change. One of the largest collaborative engagement efforts in this regard is the CA100+ initiative, which has up until recently focused on increasing disclosure and gently encouraging companies to develop transition plans. This initiative has come under increasing criticism and pressure to escalate its efforts to reflect the urgency of the situation as some major fossil fuel companies continue to expand their fossil fuel extraction capex spending, despite more than 6 years of engagement activities.[5]

Another important consideration in terms of systems thinking is to consider how comfortable and willing the financial sector is to think beyond the data. The use of judgement in making investment decisions under uncertainty is a necessary and inherent part of the process, although judgement is often denied or overlooked by investors, as the assumptions have become so deeply ingrained that they are no longer called into question, they are part of the industry's accepted wisdom (Guyatt. 2006). When it comes to utilising new tools, information, frameworks, or models that require thinking outside of these accepted norms, then the level of discomfort and resistance increases. We saw evidence of that in terms of climate change risk assessments as summarised in Chapter 6, where there was a higher perceived risk of relying on such assessments to guide capital allocation decisions, people were less confident and therefore less willing to take that step.

A systems thinking approach would help to counteract these tendencies to resist new approaches and information, as investors would start with a recognition that an assessment of future risk requires consideration of the dynamic interactions within complex systems, where there may not be historical time series or past events to predict outcomes. The financial sector depends heavily on data to justify its capital allocation decisions, even though such an approach has its shortcomings; the selection of data is subjective and past events are not accurate predictions of the future (as every prospectus of a financial institution is at pains to explain). When future events are highly complex and unprecedented, as many sustainability issues are, then it is very limiting to rely too heavily on historical time series data. It is essential that investors develop the skills to think beyond data and be able to make well considered and well-informed decisions about the future. The sources and perspectives might be different to those that they are used to, new frameworks and skills might be needed to think more broadly, but this needn't be a reason to delay or avoid cultivating a deeper understanding to enrich their investment decisions.

A pilot study on systems thinking amongst asset managers (Järnberg et al, 2023) noted that "*incorporating a systems approach to assessing sustainability impacts introduces a high level of complexity into methodologies and raises requirements for extensive data collection at the company level*" (2023:4). The study considered some different approaches that investors use to manage this complexity. These included: narrowing the focus to companies that are considered most important for achieving global sustainability impacts; using complex automation techniques; and adopting more qualitative approaches to assess system-wide sustainability impacts.

The authors noted that they did not find very good examples of the latter, revealing a very important dichotomy in the context of the financial sector. As an industry, we recognise there are gaps in the data, that data alone cannot and does not explain the complexity of the system that we make investment decisions in, yet we resist moving into territory that goes beyond overreliance on historical data. It is as though qualitative analysis is not considered worthy, or is not sufficiently robust, despite a long history of strong research and utilisation of qualitative research techniques in many disciplines of academic research and industry. As Reinecke et al (2016) noted, qualitative methods are well poised to understand and explain complex and messy phenomena in sustainability research. The tools and approaches can be helpful to examine novel or emergent questions, where no or little extant theory or data exists from which to deduce testable research hypotheses.

An additional topic of relevance to systems thinking is the growing realisation of the planetary limits to economic growth that challenges the pursuit of GDP growth that has dominated the discourse of policy makers, corporations, and investors for the past 40 years. It is common sense to see that exponential economic growth in a world of rising population and finite resources is not sustainable. Moreover, rising inequality, biodiversity loss and climate change are some of the outcomes of this pursuit of growth. Yet these connections are not often made or understood within the finance sector, as almost everyone has been trained and educated to believe that GDP growth is a valid pursuit, and that the goal of maximising short term returns on investment will induce exponential growth in the aggregate stock of financial capital (Fullerton, 2014).

> *"The same planetary boundaries that dictate limits to growth also imply limits to investment, since investment fuels growth.*

The drive for exponential returns on financial capital pushed finance to shorter-term and more speculative activity at the same time as physical resource limits to growth began to impose constraints."

The drive for exponential returns on capital and infinite GDP growth therefore feed from each other, a pursuit that clearly cannot continue if we are genuine in our quest to pursue sustainable development and restore the health of the ecosystem. There is abundant literature from credible sources that proposes alternative goals that respect the planetary boundaries and align economic and financial outcomes with goals that also prioritise justice, fairness, equality, resilience, well-being, and environmental sustainability. Meadows et al published on the Limits to Growth (1972) with extensive work from esteemed economists (OECD, 2020; Stiglitz, 2012 and 2016; Boushey, 2019; Piketty, 2013; Victor, 2019; Jackson, 2018; Hickel and Kallis, 2019; and the Institute for New Economic Thinking, 2019) that challenge the existing paradigm and propose a new economic approach.

The circular economy has emerged as a practical way to shift the economic system away from a linear economy in the pursuit of economic growth, towards the objectives of reducing consumption of resources, reducing waste, increasing recycling and re-use (UNEPFI, 2020). Fullerton (2014) and Wahl (2016) proposed regenerative capitalism to go beyond minimising harm, to pro-actively reverse the damage that has been inflicted on the ecosystem, so that it can replenish and be restored back to balance, harmony and resilience. As Rimanoczy (2022) noted, this means that we need to bring economics and finance into alignment with the Laws of Nature, not to see ourselves outside of nature or for nature to be there to be manipulated or extracted, but to see ourselves as part of the natural cycle of nature.

> *"There are no linear processes in Nature: everything flows in cycles of birth, growth, death, and rebirth. Many aspects of the [human] unsustainability of the planet are a result of the misconception that we are not governed by this law of Nature.*
> Rimanoczy (2022:61)

Many financial institutions are aware of the need for a new economic approach and see the merit of systems thinking, the circular economy and regeneration economics (Thinking Ahead Institute, 2020), however, this awareness is not always reflected in day-to-day decision-making processes. Perhaps there is an assumption that enabling a paradigm shift is an issue for policy makers or academics, they see themselves as future takers rather than future makers, (Allen, 2014); or it could be seen as a side or niche activity, perhaps they are too busy getting on with their job of investing within the existing norms that prevail. On the other hand, systems thinking would lead people to think beyond those boundaries and pro-actively find ways to contribute to financing activities that support a reduction in consumption, emissions, pollution and waste, and an increase in recycling and re-using of materials, as well as activities that support the regeneration of the ecosystem.

> A systems thinker would ask themselves how their decisions, and their role, can recognise the planetary boundaries and limits that are being tested, and allocate capital in a way that would not only stop exacerbating these imbalances, but would pro-actively pursue investments that can regenerate the system. A systems thinker would not assume or hope that someone else might do something, they would see the bigger picture and their role within that, and they would act.

This means the people working inside the financial sector need to internalise systems thinking into their mental models and how they make investment decisions. At an organisational level, this might include actions such as engaging in training and education on systems thinking, hosting events and workshops on the subject, encouraging greater skills and expertise on qualitative research techniques, building internal capacity and expertise, challenging existing norms and encouraging innovation, embedding systems thinking into the culture and ethos of the organisation.

At the individual level, developing systems thinking starts with building awareness, for example reading and engaging in the wide and extensive literature and research that exists on these topics, debating and discussing ideas and concepts with team members and colleagues, reviewing existing models and assumptions to see where systems thinking can be embedded into day-to-day frameworks, aligning investment decisions with an awareness of the planetary boundaries and a realisation that every investment decision can contribute to reducing the damage and regenerating the system as a whole.

Aligning short term decisions with long term vision

There is a body of research that focuses on the relationship between investor behaviour and the short-term investment horizon (Stein, 1989; Froot et al., 1992), with evidence to suggest that myopic behaviour prevails in the financial market (Black and Fraser, 2000; Cuthbertson et al., 1997; Miles, 1993; and Nickell and Wadhwani, 1987). Indeed, short-termism has been identified by the financial sector itself as a key barrier to action on sustainability and climate change, with Mark Carney's speech (2015) of the tragedy of the horizon being a widely cited and lauded intervention.

When we consider the remedies to short termism that have been proposed and adopted through the TCFD and other investor initiatives, we see that these mostly focus on the external conditions that prevail, rather than the internal processes that are driving the short-term investment horizon. Moreover, the discourse tends to shift away from investors needing to think with a long-term horizon and putting the onus back on to companies to do so in setting their strategy. The chicken and egg game continues, as companies complain that investors place short term pressure on them for financial performance over quarterly time horizons, so long term strategy is not rewarded or encouraged (Fuller and Jensen, 2009). Meanwhile investors advocate the need for long-term thinking, but in effect do very little to change their own mental model.

The various groups, clubs and research efforts that have looked at promoting long-term investing over the years are all largely based on the assumption that we can combat our short-term tendencies through changing the external conditions. For example, solutions include increasing the volume and reliability of information, reducing the frequency of company reports, giving long-term shareholder voting preferences, including the 'long run' in fiduciary duty laws (WBCSD, 2020). None of these deliberations consider the possibility that we could also look inwards to try to understand our behaviour and why we gravitate towards the short term. Cognitive neuroscience provides a valuable insight in this regard.
Sharot (2017) observed that it is difficult for people to think too far into the future about things that may or may not happen.

The brain likes, and is wired to be rewarded by, immediate and certain outcomes. Researchers have identified two areas of the brain that appear to compete for control over behaviour when a person attempts to balance near-term rewards with long-term goals (Woolley and Fishbach, 2017); these are emotion and abstract reasoning. Decisions involving the possibility of immediate reward activates parts of the brain influenced heavily by neural systems associated with emotion. Impulsive choices or preferences for short-term rewards result from the emotion-related parts of the brain winning out over the abstract-reasoning parts.

The remedies to cognitive limitations and short-term thinking amongst investors therefore need to go beyond external conditions such as information flow and the precise wording of legal text. We need to also contemplate how investor's appetite for short-term rewards and certainty (in a world of complexity and high uncertainty) can be managed through internal enquiry and contemplation, both at the collective (industry wide) level and for individuals. This means we need to start thinking about our intrinsic motivations, what vision we have of the future, what legacy we want to leave in the time that we have on this planet, how what we do aligns with our beliefs and sense of purpose.

By limiting ourselves to 'maximising return on investment', we not only risk oversimplification of the complex drivers of investor behaviour, but we also undermine the potential for each person to connect what they do with what matters to them, and to seek innovative solutions to sustainability challenges and problems that might arise. It is for this reason that cognitive dissonance can arise (as we will see evidence of in Chapter 6), as we become more uncomfortable with the disconnect between our beliefs, what drives us and what we do on a day-to-day basis. The wider this disconnect becomes, the level of discomfort increases, which can be a powerful point at which someone could experience a mindset shift, if they have the time, space, and motivation to make these connections.

This is why fostering a long-term mindset in finance is not only about changing the external conditions but is also about looking inside and discovering what motivates us, and what will allow each of our short-term day-to-day decisions to be consistent with the long-term vision and goals that inspire us. As psychologists Deci and Ryan (2000:54) observed, "*To be motivated means to be moved to do something.*" A person who feels energised and activated towards a certain goal is being guided by their intrinsic motivations, they are inspired to learn, to innovate and feel good about their decisions. In the context of sustainability in finance, this means that if an individual's end goal or vision is to achieve a more sustainable and prosperous future for its stakeholders, then the day-to-day decisions will be aligned with that long-term vision.

That is not to suggest that external motivations for action (such as regulations, industry standards, disclosure and reporting, bonuses and promotions) are not important, it is really to highlight that short-termism is only a problem in the financial sector when it is not consistent with long-term goals. Ideally, as Deci and Ryan (1985) argued, when intrinsic and extrinsic motivations are in alignment, then people become highly engaged, energized, curious and innovative as they are aligning their internal motivations with how they are being incentivised to behave through signals from the external world. It is at that point that people's short-term decisions would be in alignment with their long-term goals, as there is a greater sense of connection and awareness between the short and long term.

> When we think about fostering a long-term, sustainable mindset, we need to pause to consider what motivate us, what makes us feel inspired, creative, and passionate. When we connect that to our day-to-day decisions, then our short-term actions will be in alignment with our longer-term goals.

In terms of the practical implications for the finance sector and the pursuit of sustainability, it is important that when we aspire to invest sustainably and shift the investment horizon to the long-term, that we recognise that this is as much about internal alignment with that goal as it is about external incentives. If a person feels passionate about sustainability issues but the signals that they get from the organisation are that this needs to be contained, then they could feel a sense of internal conflict and be unsure how to make decisions that are consistent with those competing signals on a day-to-day basis. The short-term decisions may very well contradict or conflict with the long term in that situation.

In a situation where a person feels passionate about sustainability issues and the culture of the organisation and behaviour of others reinforce that pursuit, then there will be a greater sense of harmony internally and inside the organisation and culture more broadly. A person in that situation is more likely to turn their mind towards any challenges or obstacles with curiosity and creativity to problem solve, rather than become disengaged or reactive.

> When it comes to embedding sustainability into the finance sector, if an organisation is serious and genuine about wanting to achieve sustainable outcomes and would like to encourage

> a long-term mindset, then more attention needs to be given to support the alignment of intrinsic and extrinsic motivations of its people.

At an organisational level, this might include actions such as reviewing the design of HR policies, hiring and performance review processes, training and education programs and organisational culture. Questions that individuals might ask themselves as part of this process include: What sustainability issues am I most passionate about? What sort of world do I want to envision and want to help create through how I allocate capital? Am I comfortable that my day-to-day decisions reflect my longer-term vision? If there are conflicts or uncertainties along the way, have I searched for possible solutions or ways to address this?

Behaviours – how we behave

We have already seen the growing body of literature that shows evidence of so-called 'irrational' behaviour amongst investors (when compared to what traditional theory predicts in terms of behaviour). This body of knowledge has emerged from the behavioural finance, social psychology and economic psychology disciplines and is important for the study of the sustainability mindset principles, as it goes to the heart of acknowledging some of the limitations of existing theories and our mental models, so that we might move closer to achieving behaviour that is more aligned with the financial sector serving others and allocating capital to where it is most needed.

Some examples of this literature include the evidence of overconfidence, whereby investors overestimate the precision of their information signal (Tversky and Kahneman 1974; Cosmides and Tooby, 1996; Shefrin and Statman, 1994). This is related to the studies on over- and under-reaction (De Bondt and Thaler, 1985) where it has been shown that investors tend to overvalue the best stocks and undervalue the worst, which in turn, is usually driven by an extrapolation of recent performance (De Bondt, 1993; Shleifer and Vishny, 1990).

Evidence of herding has also been found in mutual funds (Grinblatt et al., 1995; Wermers, 1999) and in pension funds (Lakonishok et al., 1992; Nosfinger and Sias, 1999), indicating that investors tend to conform to the industry norms and mimic the behaviour of others. Finally, Shiller (2000) studied the prevalence and drivers of fads and fashions and excess volatility that pervade the market over time, suggesting that we can make quick decisions that perpetuate extreme market outcomes in times of higher uncertainty.

We have already discussed the broader context and original of theories that rely on rationality, and the limitations of such conceptualisations when it comes to understanding how people make decisions. In this discussion, rather than treat such tendencies as biases that need to be corrected to conform to a theory of rationality that is not valid in the real world, we treat this evidence as pieces of a puzzle to help us better understand the complexity of the human condition.

Two of the behavioural tendencies of particular interest in the context of sustainability and the financial sector are first, the tendency to conform to industry and organisational norms (which can give rise to resistance to change the status quo or a preference to anchor to what people know and understand). Second, the workplace culture of the financial sector can be fast-paced, competitive and stressful, giving rise to behaviours and outcomes that are tangential to achieving a more sustainable and purposeful financial system.

Encouraging innovation

An important consideration in the context of understanding investor behaviour is the extent to which investors conform to the dominant paradigm that prevails within the financial sector, which can lead to a type of groupthink that reinforces the status quo at the organisation, industry, and market-wide level. This tendency towards conformist behaviour is underpinned by so-called 'conventions' Guyatt (2006), defined as the modus operandi that guide behaviour in the face of uncertainty and external scrutiny, bringing together implicit and explicit shared beliefs and overt signals that frame expectations and interactions, both within an institution and across the financial market.

This is relevant in the context of cultivating a sustainable mindset in finance, as conventions have been shown to produce a regularity in behaviour that is based on the expectations of others' behaviour and for which it is mutually beneficial to co-ordinate in different situational contexts (either consciously or unconsciously). It means that a form of groupthink about what is legitimate and justifiable to others can result in over reliance on narrow investment criteria and sources of information, solidifying the status quo and making it hard to incorporate wider issues related to sustainability and climate change that sit outside the boundaries of deep acceptance.

As Chapter 2 illustrated, we are seeing a change in some industry conventions that are allowing sustainability considerations to enter the mainstream discourse of finance, such as the inclusion of sustainability in investment belief statements, setting goals and objectives that incorporate sustainability outcomes, and increased focus on engaging with governments and investee companies to promote more sustainable behaviour. However, we have also seen the prevalence of greenwashing, the persistent gap between the financial sector's aspirations and its capital allocation decisions, and a failure to internalise a broader definition of the purpose of finance.

These are all indicative of an industry that is still anchoring to dominant conventions that have not yet shifted on the fundamentals of finance. As the industry embarks on the journey of learning and evolving its processes and thinking, the strength of beliefs and internalisation of a broader sense of purpose are crucial parts of building new industry conventions that will move the industry towards a more genuine sustainability position.

Challenging and changing existing industry conventions also requires an element of courage and willingness to overlook the perceived risk of doing something different from the norm (Chapter 6). What this means in practice, is that financial institutions need to be willing to internalise a deeper sense of purpose that relates to its context and stakeholders, to bring a closer connection between legal duties, a broader sense of purpose and connection to individual and organisational beliefs.

It also means that financial institutions need to encourage and promote innovation and creativity as part of the investment process,

framed by this greater sense of purpose that embeds sustainability beliefs and the intrinsic motivations of its employees.
Financial innovation is prolific and there is certainly a lot of creativity inside the sector that has delivered positive social and environmental benefits (IMF, 2021), although this potential is not always harnessed in a way that reflects a broader sense of purpose that goes beyond making money in the short term, to one that is aligned with societal values and long-term interests. While not a silver bullet, a clearly defined broader sense of purpose at the industry, organisational and individual level would certainly help to form these connections and better guide the finance sector's day-to-day decisions.

In this way, challenging existing conventions through innovation could result in short-term decisions that are more likely to be consistent with longer term sustainability goals, and not lead to unethical behaviour if driven only by an unbridled profit motive. The financial imperative remains the overarching goal, but what is occurring is a deeper connection between how the financial returns and profits are generated as being just as important as the outcome itself.

At the organisational level, financial institutions can create a culture whereby investors are encouraged to seek new ways to think and alternative sources of information and perspectives, to challenge the status quo. There are many ways to approach innovation, for example establishing an innovation centre (APG, n.d.) or setting a strategic goal to promote innovation and aligning this with the broader sense of purpose and sustainability goals (Nidumolu et al, 2009).

> It is important to establish a link between achieving sustainability objectives and promoting innovation, to encourage pro-active problem solving and exploration of new ways of seeing and doing things beyond the existing norms and conventions. That is fundamental to cultivating a sustainable mindset in finance, as existing norms can narrow how investors think, limiting their creative potential to seek solutions to problems or challenges that are new or unprecedented.

Some questions for investors to consider as part of the day-to-day investment decisions might include: If the data and traditional financial metrics do not provide sufficient information on the sustainability impacts, have I sought alternative sources and perspectives? If I encounter challenges or conflicting signals when considering sustainability issues as part of my decisions, do I look for solutions to these or think of different ways to tackle the issue? What new approaches have I developed and implemented to incorporate sustainability into my investment decisions?

Promoting mindfulness, health and well-being

Many people in the financial sector find themselves working in a high pressured, competitive, and stressful environment that prioritises quick decisions and short-term gains. This environment can encourage people to make decisions quickly, which can give rise to automatic decisions (Systems 1 thinking) and reinforce the tendency to conform to existing structures and knowledge.

What this fast paced and competitive environment can also result in is increased stress and behaviour that leads to burnout – a state of physical and emotional exhaustion. While burnout is often discussed in different contexts to the pursuit of sustainability, it is a symptom of the same set of conditions. Let me explain a little further.

Research in the UK found that 58% of financial services professionals feel that their life is out of control, and that 46% admit there are times they've felt like running away, highlighting their fragile mental state (Glasspool, 2022). A poor workplace culture has been found to increase moderate to severe burnout by 157%, this includes lack of organisational purpose, few opportunities to grow and develop, poor teamwork and a control and command leadership approach.

What this means is that the combination of a competitive and fast paced environment, along with a lack of belief in why people are doing what they are doing and lack of agency over what they are doing, can result in higher levels of stress and potential burnout. This is about how we behave as an industry, the culture and norms that prevail, and the decisions that we make as we try to perform in that context.

We can clearly see a dilemma here in terms of how the culture in the finance sector potentially undermines the pursuit of sustainability. To create a kinder, more thoughtful world that does not pursue short term gain and create undue stress (on people and the planet), we need to embody this goal as part of our day-to-day interactions with each other, and the prevailing culture of the industry. It will be very difficult for the finance sector to create a sustainable financial system if it is coming from a place of unsustainability and disregard for the health and well-being of the people who work inside the industry.

Putting this another way, when people are healthy, feel a sense of purpose and agency, then they are more likely to be motivated to act with greater care, and have the energy and vitality to make positive change.

> Sustainability is not a goal to be pursued 'out there' while we carry on working in ways that are highly stressful and unkind to ourselves, to each other and to the planet. By creating a workplace and industry culture that embodies sustainability into how it thinks and behaves, we will find that we naturally give more regard to our own health, to the health of others and of course, to the health and sustainability of the entire ecosystem.

At the organisational level, this has many implications that start from the top of the organisation and the culture that the management want to create and perpetuate. The targets and key performance indicators need to recognise and reflect the health and wellbeing of its staff and instil a sense of care and respect for each other. There are some emerging examples of wellbeing programs in financial organisations, in part a response to the burnout trends and the stress created by the aftermath of Covid-19.

The practice of mindfulness has been utilised to help create this cultural transformation in a broad array of contexts, with Boschert et al (2020) developing some resources and case studies to illustrate how this works in practice in the financial sector. Boschert et al define mindfulness as "*the ability to regulate attention, emotions and awareness,*" (2020:4) to not only address stress and reduce burnout risk, but to also strengthen conscious decision-making and change entrenched habits. The research noted that mindfulness training can be helpful for the financial sector, as cultivation of *"attention regulation, emotional and body awareness, positive outlook and meta-awareness"* (2020:22) are core skills to improve wellbeing and to foster innovation and collaboration as we move towards a more just and sustainable financial system.

An additional element of mindfulness that is relevant for financial institutions and sustainability is to allow time and space to tap into our inner wisdom or intuition. The role of wisdom as part of systems thinking was discussed earlier, where we saw that wisdom embodies not only the accumulation of knowledge and understanding about the external world, but also how our inner conditions influence how we understand the interconnections and react to such stimuli. Inner wisdom is often likened to gut instinct, or the inner voice, that feeling that we get when we are guided by something that is not completely explainable, but it feels right. In the context of finance, our inner wisdom might be confused as being a behavioural bias, a Systems 1 automatic response aka the Kahneman model of behaviour. However, as Waddock (2010) argues, inner wisdom is much more powerful than our automatic reactions, it is those moments when we may have some evidence, facts, opinions, and past decision patterns – but something else is guiding us towards a certain outcome or behaviour, and that something is our broader systems perspective and sense of ethics and morality. This will vary from person to person and across different cultural contexts, what the inner wisdom is telling us specifically is less important than creating space to listen to it.

At the organisational level, the practical implications of the link between mindfulness, inner wisdom, well-being, and conscious decision making that can support and enable a sustainable mindset shift are wide and varied. Boschert et al (2020:22-23) provide some examples of actions that have been taken within the financial sector, including: prioritising employee wellbeing and trust inside an organisation and through client and stakeholder relationships, undertaking training on mindfulness (both the management and team members), identifying the internal champions or people who are enthusiastic about mindfulness or already practicing it in their personal lives to be key agents for change internally, and daily meditation practice as a team and individually to begin to normalise and reinforce the habit and culture of engaging in mindful practice.

Some questions that individuals could ask themselves to link this reflective practice with their day-to-day investment decisions might include: Have I paused to reflect on the wider consequences of this decision for the environment, or for communities that might be impacted? How do I feel about those potential impacts? Is there an element of uncertainty and judgement that I am applying, and if so, what am I assuming? Could I look at these issues differently? Are there other sources of information or expertise I could consider? Are there alternative investments that might generate comparable financial returns with greater benefits for communities and/or the environment?

> We can see the clear synergies between each of the elements of the literature that have been considered in relation to cultivating a sustainable mindset in finance. Mindfulness and inner wisdom will help to guide the: internalisation of

a broader sense of purpose; realisation and connection to our beliefs; alignment between our short-term decisions and long-term vision; understanding the interlinkages and impact our decisions have on real world outcomes through systems thinking; and the courage to resist conventions and seek innovative solutions when challenges arise.

A sustainability mindset framework for finance

To help facilitate this process of deeper, inner inquiry from within the financial sector and bring together the insights from the prevailing research and literature, a summary of suggested actions for the finance sector are set out in Figure 8, referred to as the 'Sustainability Mindset Framework for Finance'.

The sustainability mindset principles have been interpreted and re-grouped to align with the decision-making flow for financial institutions, also reflecting the relevant literature in the context of the financial sector. The framework sets out some suggested actions and issues for the finance sector to consider (and pitfalls to avoid) that emanate from each of these areas, with a summary of some key questions highlighted in Figure 9.

Any organisation or individual working inside the financial sector that has a sustainability goal or policy will benefit from examining the prevailing mindsets, to help identify the barriers to change and close the gaps between aspirations and actions. In addition, any policy maker or regulator can utilise the mindsets framework to encourage the wider industry to look more closely at their mental models and how they think. This will ultimately help to build a financial system that is safer, more sustainable, and ethically sound. A financial industry with a broader sense of purpose.

Figure 8. Highlights of the Sustainable Mindset for Finance Framework

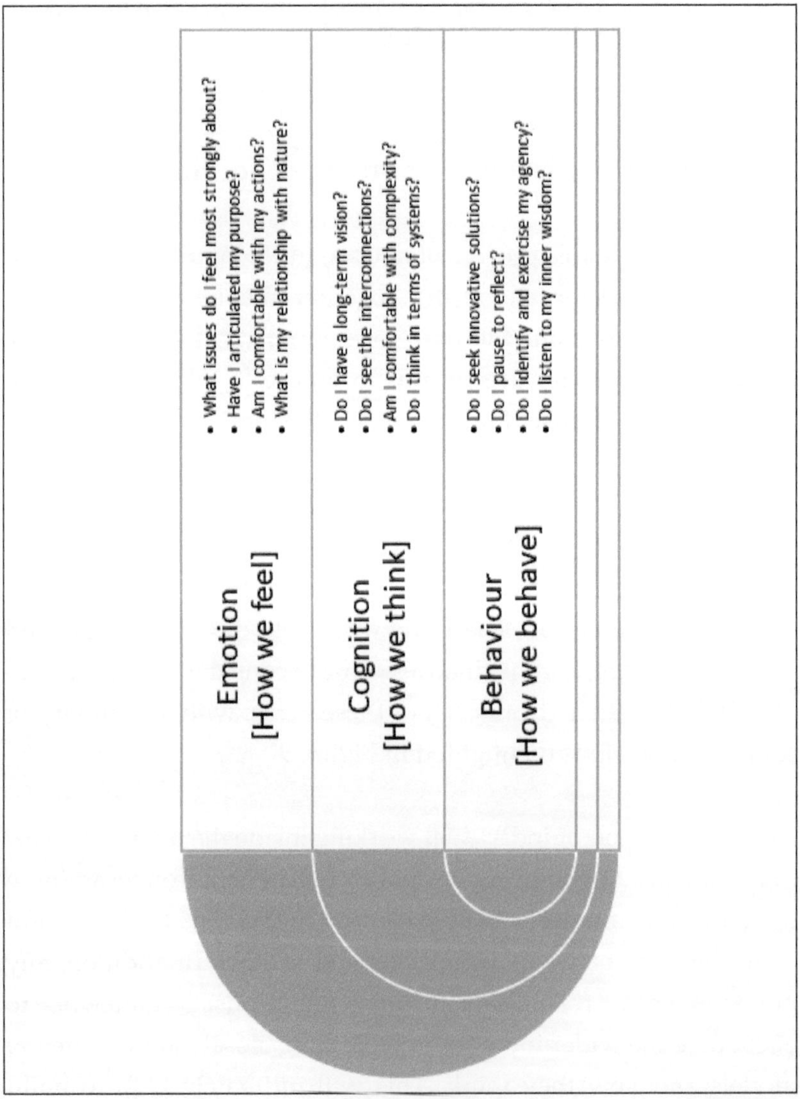

Figure 9. Sustainability Mindset Framework for the Finance Sector

Sustainability Mindset Principle	**Suggested Actions for the Financial Sector**	**Possible questions to ask**	**Pitfalls to avoid**
Emotion – How we feel			
Ecoliteracy ***What issues do I feel most strongly about?***	Build knowledge and articulate sustainability priorities to incorporate into investment beliefs and decision-making frameworks.	How concerned am I about sustainability? What sustainability issues am I most passionate about? Are there any examples of sustainability actions that I have seen or heard about that I find inspiring? How do I reflect my concerns / passions into my investment beliefs and how I make investment decisions? What are the industries and activities that I think will thrive and prosper in the future? Where do the greatest risks and opportunities lie?	Lack of time available to learn and build knowledge about sustainability issues, or to connect with our own feelings about the issues. Assume the sustainability 'experts' or others will take care of these issues, rather than seeing it as a role for everybody. Seeing sustainability beliefs as separate to core investment beliefs. Looking at the issues from a purely intellectual understanding, with no personal connection to the issues.

Purpose ***Have I articulated my purpose?***	Articulate the reason why the organisation exists, who it serves and what needs it fulfills, what that means to you personally, and how embedding sustainability is integral to fulfilling this purpose.	What is my organisation's purpose? What does that mean to me personally? How does this relate to the issues that I feel most passionately about? Whose needs am I serving? What are my clients / beneficiaries' needs? Have I considered the broader context that also impacts on the lives of my clients / beneficiaries? How do my investment decisions best serve these needs?	Defining purpose narrowly as 'making money' or 'generating returns' when these are outcomes, they do not explain why the organisation exists. Failure to recognise that the broader context impacts on the clients/ beneficiaries lives and the role that finance play in achieving those favourable conditions (e.g., financial stability, fairness, justice, diversity, clean air, water, healthy environment).

My contribution ***Am I comfortable with my actions?***	Consider how you feel about your contribution to the sustainability problems and / or solutions, aligning these to your beliefs and purpose.	Who / what will be impacted by the company's activities? Do the positives outweigh the negatives? How do I feel about any potential harmful effects from this investment? Are there alternative companies or assets with good financial prospects and positive outcomes for society and the environment? What are the likely industries and activities that will support sustainable outcomes? Can I allocate more capital to these activities?	Considering sustainability issues as a niche investment opportunity set. Failing to connect or experience emotional reactions, as a way to guide decisions that are more aligned to beliefs and purpose. Assuming that there might be lower investment return on assets that also deliver positive real-world impact, without conducting the analysis. Not being aware of (or failing to seek out) alternative investments that would also deliver a more positive sustainability impact.

Oneness with nature ***What is my relationship with nature?***	Consider your connection to nature and how that can be reflected in your investment decisions on a day-to-day basis.	Do I feel part of nature, or separate to it? How does nature relate to my role as an investor? Are there experiences in my life when I have felt connected to nature that I can draw from when I am contemplating an investment? When I look at investments that might harm others or the natural world, have I considered alternatives that might be beneficial rather than harmful? Can I allocate more capital to the companies or industries whose activities will help to protect and restore nature?	Seeing themselves as outside of nature, not part of it. Being able to recall experiences of feeling connected to nature, but not seeing how this is relevant to their role as an investor. Assuming that compliance with environmental regulations is sufficient to preserve the natural environment. Assuming that there is a trade-off between preserving nature and financial returns. Not pro-actively looking for investments that will help to preserve and regenerate the natural world.

Cognition – How we think			
Long-term thinking ***Do I have a long-term vision?***	Consider the potential long-term implications before making an investment decision, including the wider social and environmental impacts.	How would I like the world to be in 10 years from now? Is this investment decision enabling that vision? What time horizon have I considered as part of my investment due diligence? What impact will the investment have on future generations and the natural world? Am I contributing to a more sustainable future with this investment?	Looking at the issues with a short-term lens, where financial metrics could dominate or cloud judgement over wider impacts. Assuming that the future is too uncertain to evaluate, hence focus on the short term as that is the most comfortable and what others are doing. Failing to explore the dynamic connections between actions and long-term outcomes at the system wide level.

Interconnectedness ***Do I see the interconnections?***	Build an understanding of the interconnections, linkages and interactions between investment decisions and real-world outcomes, from different perspectives.	Have I considered how this investment might impact on the integrity and stability of the financial system overall? Have I identified any possible unintended consequences on society, the natural world or the system as a whole? Have I considered the extent to which this investment will flow on to benefit others or the broader environment?	Failing to understand that they are not passive participants in the financial system but that their decisions influence the level of risk and stability of the system. Viewing decisions in isolation and not considering the knock-on consequences for others or the functioning of the system as a whole. Seeing investment decisions as a zero-sum game and downplaying the connections within and between the financial sector and real-world outcomes.

Both+ and thinking ***Am I comfortable with complexity?***	Build an understanding of the uncertainties and complexities to guide investment decisions, exercising judgement and seeking divergent perspectives.	How much of this investment decision is based on historical data and information? Is there a degree of uncertainty that requires me to form a judgement that is not entirely based on data? How have I responded to the uncertainties in relation to the asset's potential sustainability impact? Are there any trade-offs that I can foresee in terms of the impact that this investment could have on society, the natural world, or the wider system? If yes, how am I managing these potential trade-offs?	Not seeing the nuances in how risks and opportunities inter-relate and the creative aspect of exercising judgement under uncertainty. Utilising narrow criteria and sources that align with the status quo, assuming the past cycles will repeat. Avoid examining or contemplating the nuances and complexities, using that as a rationale for putting sustainability in the 'too hard' basket. Feeling uncomfortable with complexity and multiple solutions.

Flow in cycles ***Do I think in terms of systems?***	Consider how much the investment decisions rely on the assumption of infinite economic growth and explore the potential impact of alternative economic models.	Have I considered what would happen to this company and/or asset if economic growth was no longer a viable pursuit or outcome? How resilient would the asset be in a circular economy, where finite resources reward behaviours, products and services that minimise consumption, resource usage and waste and encourage recycling and regeneration? What other companies and/or assets can I consider that would thrive in a circular economy where regeneration proliferated?	Assuming that economic growth will continue indefinitely as one of the underpinnings for financial analysis. Failure to consider and seek out investment opportunities that might prosper in a world that is more focused on preserving and minimising use of finite resources. Existing models and networks that fail to challenge the presumption of infinite growth as a viable basis to conduct financial analysis.

Behavioural response – How we behave			
Creative innovation ***Do I seek innovative solutions?***	Consider new approaches and innovations to incorporate sustainability issues into investment processes.	If the data and traditional financial metrics do not provide sufficient information on the sustainability impacts, have I sought alternative sources and perspectives? If I encounter challenges or conflicting signals when considering sustainability issues as part of my decisions, do I look for solutions to these or think of different ways to tackle the issue? What new approaches have I developed and implemented to incorporate sustainability into my investment decisions?	Waiting for perfect data and information on sustainability impacts before incorporating such considerations into investment decisions. Overreliance on historical information that aligns with existing paradigms and business models, without challenging the status quo or being creative in adapting to the changing investment landscape. Assuming that if an issue doesn't easily fit into existing models then it cannot be considered, rather than questioning how existing models could be adapted.

Reflection ***Do I pause to reflect?***	Allow sufficient space and time to question assumptions and explore the complexities before making an investment decision.	Have I paused to reflect on the wider consequences of this investment for the environment or communities that might be adversely impacted? How do I feel about those potential impacts? Are there other sources of information or expertise I could draw from? Have I looked for other investments that would generate more positive social and environmental benefits?	Making decisions quickly, defaulting to the widely relied upon sources of information, data and rationale for such decisions. Being 'too busy' to step back to consider the wider ramifications of the investment. Working long hours with high levels of stress can lead to poor health and Systems 1 automatic thinking can take over.

Self-awareness ***Do I identify and exercise my agency?***	Consider how each investment decision could potentially impact on real-world outcomes and reflect on how you want to use that influence.	Have I identified the different ways that I can exercise my influence as an investor, in a way that aligns with my beliefs and broader sense of purpose? Do I feel empowered to act on the sustainability issues that I consider to be important, where I feel I can have the greatest impact? Can I pause to recognise when a decision or action might be driven by external pressures and adherence prevailing norms and try to formulate an alternative response?	Not identifying how they can exercise their influence, or failing to think about the specific actions that they can take. Assuming that conforming to the wisdom of the crowd is the best (and only) way to perform their investment duties. Automatically reverting to existing norms, data sources, economic models and assumptions when challenges arise.

Mindfulness – ***Do I listen to my intuition?***	Consider your inner guide and voice to ascertain any reaction of discomfort or comfort, before making investment decisions.	Can I pause to consider how a particular investment decision or action feels before proceeding? Do I feel comfort, discomfort, or something else? Have I checked back to my beliefs and broader sense of purpose to see how the investment aligns with that? As I pause to reflect, is there a feeling of conflict, or does the decision feel 'right'? Could I make a different decision, that would reduce the feeling of conflict and better align with my broader sense of purpose?	Confusing inner wisdom with automatic responses, that are made quickly with little space for reflection. Feeling stressed and tired and not realising that this could be an expression of the body's discomfort with certain behaviours and decisions. Not trusting inner wisdom, or assuming that this is for personal life decisions and not relevant for the workplace. Not taking the time to check in and see if there is an emotional or physical response that could help to make a better decision.

It is suggested that the application of the mindset framework be carried out through a facilitated team setting or for individual contemplation, by simply thinking about each of the questions and issues raised and extending the enquiry further where needed, depending on what issues arise and where the greatest potential for development might be. It could also be included as part of an organisation's board, committee and staff training and development programs.

There are four suggested stages to help steer this process, namely:

1. Define the objective – what are we trying to achieve?
2. Identify the barriers – what are the main challenges in achieving this objective?
3. Apply the mindset framework – can the sustainable mindset lens help us approach these challenges differently?
4. Reflect and respond – what key insights and next steps emerged from this process?

To illustrate how this framework can be applied and to contribute to our collective knowledge on a prescient topic, the framework is applied to consider the goal of closing the climate financing gap by allocating private sector capital to where it is most needed with the urgency that is required. Chapters 5 and 6 consider the external and internal barriers to mobilising capital, with Chapter 7 examining these barriers through a sustainable mindset lens.

Summary

This chapter has explored some of the literature related to mindsets, the sustainability mindsets principles and the emotional, cognitive, and behavioural influences on investor decision making. The chapter has argued that it will be harder (but not impossible) for people with a fixed mindset to want to adapt to an enlarged sense of purpose that embeds sustainability at its core. While people with a growth mindset will be more open to change and willing to adapt, they may not have aligned their personal beliefs and motivations with sustainability goals, or they may be unsure about what it means in practice and still have some way to go before that goal can be realised.

This is why the sustainability mindset principles are valuable, as they take that next step to explicitly consider what mindset characteristics will best align with achieving the broader goals of sustainability. The 12 sustainable mindset principles have been applied to the specific context of the finance sector, to guide the process of self-examination and exploration at the individual and organisational level, to look closer at the inner workings of the people and see if there is a different way to respond to the complexities and opportunities for transformation that the sustainability challenge presents. From this process, a sustainable mindsets framework for finance has been developed and presented across the three pillars of Emotion (how we feel), Cognition (how we think) and Behaviour (how we behave).

In terms of the emotional characteristics of a sustainability mindset, we explored the limitations of the neoclassical notion of rational homo economicus and looked at how emotions could be harnessed to support the integration of sustainability issues into investment decisions in a more genuine way. Rather than ignoring our emotions, pretending they don't play a role in investment decisions, or indeed treating them as a behavioural bias that needs to be corrected, we could also look at how emotions could be part of the transformation process. When we connect our head with our heart, anything is possible. There are many ways to approach this, and there is a raft of literature and examples of the practical application of building emotional intelligence that we can draw from. The discussion suggested two key areas specific to the investment context – that is embracing a broader sense of purpose of the finance sector, and the realisation and alignment with our beliefs.

Harnessing our emotions goes beyond crafting tweaks to a legal text on fiduciary duty or an investment belief statement that is imposed on people by others. It means we need to step back and asking questions differently (at the individual and organisational level), such as: Do we believe that a more secure, safer, and prosperous world will be beneficial for our stakeholders and the people whose needs we are serving? Do we believe that we can help to create that world through our capital allocation decisions? Where is capital most needed to provide a secure, safe, and prosperous world now and into the future? How can we accelerate our allocation to capital to these areas with the urgency that is required?

In turning to how investors think (cognition), we explored some of the behavioural and psychological literature that further challenges the notion of rationality, as the evidence shows that investors are at risk of repeating cognitive errors and biases, are easily manipulated, and riven by sometimes irrational beliefs and fears. This is an important body of work in the context of the finance sector, as it goes to the heart of how capital can be misallocated at the global level, and it also helps to explain why sustainability issues can be overlooked or relegated to the 'too hard' basket, as it is still relatively new to investors and would therefore take more Systems 2 thinking effort (aka Kahneman). Two of the areas that warrant closer attention in relation to cognitive processes and the ability of the financial sector to support and enable the shift to a sustainable financial system are: 1) the need to develop systems thinking within the finance sector to combat reductionist and narrow framing, and 2) to align short-term investment decisions with long-term vision, such that our urge for short term rewards and actions is steered towards (and in alignment with) the long term vision of the sustainable future we see.

A systems thinker would ask themselves how their decisions, and their role, can recognise the planetary boundaries and limits that are being tested, and allocate capital in a way that would not only stop exacerbating these imbalances, but would pro-actively pursue investments that can regenerate the system. A systems thinker does not assume or hope that someone else will do something, they see the bigger picture and their role within that, and they act. This means the financial sector needs to internalise systems thinking into their mental models and how they make investment decisions. At an organisational level, this might include actions such as engaging in training and education on systems thinking, hosting events and workshops on the subject, encouraging greater skills and expertise on qualitative research techniques, building internal capacity and expertise, challenging existing norms and encouraging innovation, embedding systems thinking into the culture and ethos of the organisation.

At the individual level, developing systems thinking starts with building awareness, for example reading and engaging in the wide and extensive literature and research that exists on these topics, debating and discussing ideas and concepts with team members and colleagues, reviewing existing models and assumptions to see where systems thinking can be embedded into day-to-day frameworks, aligning investment decisions with an awareness of the planetary boundaries and a realisation that every single investment decision can contribute to reducing the damage and regenerating the system as a whole (where we are part of the whole, not separate to it).

When we think about fostering a long-term, sustainable mindset, we need to pause to consider what motivate us, what makes us feel inspired, creative, and passionate. When we connect that to our day-to-day decisions, then our short-term actions will be in alignment with longer-term goals. This means that if an organisation is serious and genuine about wanting to achieve sustainable outcomes and would like to encourage a long-term mindset, then more attention needs to be given to support the alignment of intrinsic and extrinsic motivations of its people. At an organisational level, this might include actions such as reviewing the design of HR policies, hiring and performance review processes, training and education programs and organisational culture. Questions that individuals might ask themselves as part of this process include: What sustainability issues am I most passionate about? What sort of world do I want to envision and want to help create through how I allocate capital? Am I comfortable that my day-to-day decisions reflect my longer-term vision? If there are conflicts or uncertainties along the way, have I searched for possible solutions or ways to address this?

Finally, in terms of how investors behave, we have already seen the growing body of literature that shows evidence of so-called 'irrational' behaviour amongst investors (when compared to what traditional theory predicts in terms of behaviour). This body of knowledge is important for the study of the sustainability mindset in finance, as it goes to the heart of acknowledging some of the limitations of existing theories and our mental models, so that we might move closer to achieving behaviour that is more aligned with the financial sector serving others and allocating capital to where it is most needed. Two of the behavioural tendencies of particular interest are first, the tendency to conform to industry and organisational norms (which can give rise to resistance to change the status quo or a preference to anchor to what people know and understand). Second, the workplace culture of the financial sector can be fast-paced, competitive and stressful, giving rise to behaviours and outcomes that are tangential to achieving a more sustainable and purposeful financial system.

One of the antidotes to the observed tendency to conform to industry norms that can undermine sustainability actions in the finance sector is to encourage a culture of innovation, whereby innovation is aligned to a broader sense of purpose and vision for the future. What this means in practice, is that financial institutions need to encourage and promote innovation and creativity as part of the investment process, framed by a greater sense of purpose that embeds sustainability beliefs and the intrinsic motivations of its employees. In this way, challenging existing conventions through innovation could result in short-term decisions that are more likely to be consistent with longer term sustainability goals, and not lead to unethical behaviour if only driven by an unbridled profit motive. The financial imperative remains the overarching goal, but what is occurring is a deeper connection between HOW the financial returns and profits are generated as being just as important as the outcome itself.

One of the most important things is to establish a link between achieving sustainability objectives and promoting innovation, to encourage pro-active problem solving and exploration of new ways of seeing and doing things beyond the existing norms and conventions. That is fundamental to cultivating a sustainable mindset in finance, as existing norms can narrow how investors think, limiting their creative potential to seek solutions to problems or challenges that are new or unprecedented (and sustainability issues certainly fall into this category).

A suggested antidote to the fast-paced, stressful, and competitive culture of the finance sector that can give rise to unsustainable behaviours is to promote mindfulness, health, and well-being. Sustainability then becomes a pursuit that is not treated as a goal 'out there' while we carry on working in ways that are highly stressful and unkind to ourselves, to each other and to the planet. By creating a workplace and industry culture that embodies sustainability into how it thinks and behaves, we will find that we naturally give more regard to our own health, to the health of others and of course, to the health and sustainability of the entire ecosystem. This means slowing down, pausing, and listening to our inner wisdom to assess if our behaviour on a day-to-day basis feels right, is it in alignment with our broader sense of purpose and vision for the future?

We can see the clear synergies between each of the elements of the literature that has been considered in presenting a framework to help cultivate a sustainable mindset in finance. Mindfulness and inner wisdom will help to guide the internalisation of a broader sense of purpose, realisation and connection to our beliefs, alignment between our short-term decisions and long-term vision, an understanding of the interlinkages and impact our decisions have on real world outcomes through systems thinking, and the courage to resist conventions and seek innovative solutions when challenges arise.

The framework calls upon the financial sector to engage in the process of learning and enquiry, to consider sustainability issues from a different perspective and to ask different questions of themselves at a more personal level. It is not a new rulebook for people to follow, or a new mantra to repeat. Rather, it is a framework to support the process of internal enquiry that could enable a more rapid acceleration of actions that support sustainable outcomes, simply by taking the time to look at how we think.

We will now examine the climate financing gap that exists to achieve Net Zero by 2050 and climate resilience, before turning to apply the mindsets framework to consider alternative perspectives on how the gap can be closed with the urgency that is required.

References

Ackoff, R.L. (2004). Transforming the systems movement. Political Science.

Allen, J. (2014). Long-term thinking. An article published by Bain & Company.

APG. (n.d.) Innovation Manual, Volume 9. An internal innovation manual published by the Dutch pension fund APG.

Aristotle 980a Metaphysics, Translated by W. D. Ross.

Atwater, J. B., Kannan, V. R., & Stephens, A. A. (2008). Cultivating Systemic Thinking in the Next Generation of Business Leaders. Academy of Management Learning & Education, 7(1), 9–25. http://www.jstor.org/stable/40214494

Aviva Investors. (2022). The levers of change: A systems approach to reconcile finance with planetary boundaries. An article published by Global Investment Thinking, Aviva Investors.

Baggio, A., Digentiki, E., and Varma, R. (2019). Organizations do not change. People change! McKinsey & Company. People and organisational performance. https://www.mckinsey.com/capabilities/people-and-organizational-performance/our-insights/the-organization-blog/organizations-do-not-change-people-change

Basford, T., and Schaninger, B. (2016). The four building blocks of change. An article published by McKinsey Quarterly.

BCI (n.d.) Beliefs are important to our success. Published by the British Columbia Investment Management Corporation, Canada.

Black, A. & Fraser, P. (2002). Stock market short-termism - An international perspective. Journal of Multinational Financial Management. Vol.12(2):135-158.

Boushey, H. (2019). Unbound: How Inequality Constricts Our Economy and What We Can Do About It. Harvard University Press.

Bouzguenda, K. (2018). Emotional intelligence and financial decision making: Are we talking about a paradigmatic shift or a change in practices? Research in International Business and Finance, Elsevier, vol. 44(C), pages 273-284.

Boschert, F., Höppner, K., Rupprecht, S., and Tamdjidi, C. (2020). Mindset Change for Transformation in Finance: What creates sustainable cultural transformation? A report published by the Mindful Finance Institute.

Carney, M. (2015). BIS central bankers' speeches Mark Carney: Breaking the tragedy of the horizon -climate change and financial stability. Available at: https://www.bis.org/review/r151009a.pdf.

Cosmides, L., & Tooby, J. (1996). Are humans good intuitive statisticians after all? Rethinking some conclusions from the literature on judgment under uncertainty. Cognition, 58(1), 1–73. https://doi.org/10.1016/0010-0277(95)00664-8.

Cuthbertson, K., Hayes, S., & Nitzsche, D. (1997). The Behaviour of UK Stock Prices and Returns: Is the Market Efficient? The Economic Journal, 107(443), 986–1008. http://www.jstor.org/stable/2957845.

Damasio, A. R. (1994). Descartes' Error: Emotion Reason, and the Human Brain. New York: Avon Books.

Daniel, K.D., Hirshleifer, D.A. and Teoh, S.H. (2001). Investor Psychology in Capital Markets: Evidence and Policy Implications. SSRN Electronic Journal. doi:https://doi.org/10.2139/ssrn.278848.

De Bondt, Werner. (1993), Betting on trends: Intuitive forecasts of financial risk and return, International Journal of Forecasting, 9, issue 3, p. 355-371, https://EconPapers.repec.org/RePEc:eee:intfor:v:9:y:1993:i:3:p:355-371.

De Bondt, Werner F. M., and Thaler, R. (1985). Does the Stock Market Overreact? The Journal of Finance, 40(3), 793–805. https://doi.org/10.2307/2327804

Deci, E. L., & Ryan, R. M. (2010). Self-Determination. New York, NY: John Wiley & Sons, Inc. http;//dx.doi.org/10.1002/9780470479216.corpsy0834.

Dixon, W., and Wilson, D. (2013). A History of Homo Economicus: The Nature of the Moral in Economic Theory, Routledge.

Dweck, C. S., and Yeager, D. S. (2021). A growth mindset about intelligence. In G. M. Walton & A. J. Crum (Eds.), Handbook of wise interventions: How social psychology can help people change (pp. 9–35). The Guilford Press.

Dweck, C.S. (2017). Mindset, Updated edition, Random House.

Dweck C.S. (2012). Mindsets and malleable minds: Implications for giftedness and talent. In: Subotnik R.F., Robinson A., Callahan C.M., Gubbins E.J., editors. Malleable Minds: Translating Insights from Psychology and Neuroscience to Gifted Education. National Research Center on the Gifted and Talented, University of Connecticut; Storrs, CT, USA: 2012. pp. 7–18.

Dweck, C. S. (1975). The role of expectations and attributions in the alleviation of learned helplessness. Journal of Personality and Social Psychology, 31(4), 674–685. https://doi.org/10.1037/h0077149.

EAPF. (n.d.) Responsible Investment Makes Business Sense. A set of investment beliefs that incorporate climate change. Published by the Environment Agency Pension Fund, UK.

Froot, K.A., Scharfstein, D.S. and Stein, J.C. (1992), Herd on the Street: Informational Inefficiencies in a Market with Short-Term Speculation. The Journal of Finance, 47: 1461-1484. https://doi.org/10.1111/j.1540-6261.1992.tb04665.

Fuller, J,. and Jensen, M. (2009). 8. Just Say No to Wall Street: Putting a Stop to the Earnings Game. In D. Chew & S. Gillan (Ed.), U.S.

Corporate Governance (pp. 161-169). New York Chichester, West Sussex: Columbia University Press. https://doi.org/10.7312/chew14856-008.

Fullerton, J. (2014). Limits to Investment: Finance in the Anthropocene. An article published by the Great Transition Initiative: Towards a transformative vision and practice.

Goleman, D. (2007). Emotional Intelligence (10th ed.). Bantam Books.

Glasspool, J. (2022). Tackling burnout in financial services. An article published by IFA Magazine.

Grinblatt, M., Titman, S., and Wermers, R. (1995). Momentum Investment Strategies, Portfolio Performance, and Herding: A Study of Mutual Fund Behavior. American Economic Review, 85, 1088-1105.

Guyatt, D. (2006). Identifying and Overcoming Behavioural Impediments to Long Term Responsible Investment: A Focus on UK Institutional Investors. Available at SSRN: https://ssrn.com/abstract=1911821 or http://dx.doi.org/10.2139/ssrn.1911821.

Hickel, J. and Kallis, G. (2019). Is Green Growth Possible? New Political Economy, 1-18. https://doi.10.1080/13563467.2019.1598964.

Hirshleifer, D. (2001). Investor Psychology and Asset Pricing. The Journal of Finance, 56(4), 1533–1597. http://www.jstor.org/stable/2697808

Hodgson, T. (2017). System thinking and investment: Introducing the ecosystem perspective. Thinking Ahead Institute, Willis Towers Watson.

ICAEW. (2018). Culture and purpose in financial services. Published by ICAEW thought leadership: financial services.

IMF. (2021). From financial innovation to inclusion. An article published by the IMF.

Institute for New Economic Thinking. (2019). Is Green Growth Possible: A Debate. https://www.ineteconomics.org/perspectives/collections/is-green-growth-possible-a- debate

Jackson, T. (2018). The post-growth challenge: secular stagnation, inequality and the limits to growth, CUSP Working Paper, https://timjackson.org.uk/the-post-growth-challenge/.

Järnberg, L., Maltais, A., & Moberg, Å. (2023). A Pilot Study on Systems Thinking in Asset Management. SEI Report. Stockholm Environment Institute. https://doi.org/10.51414/sei2023.027

Kahneman, D. (2011). Thinking, fast and slow. Farrar, Straus and Giroux.

Kassel, K., Rimanoczy, I. and Mitchell, S.F. (2016). The sustainable mindset: Connecting being, thinking, and doing in management education. In Academy of management proceedings (Vol. 2016, No. 1, p. 16659). Briarcliff Manor, NY 10510: Academy of Management.

Lagarde, C. (2019). The Financial Sector: Redefining a Broader Sense of Purpose, 32nd World Traders' Tacitus Lecture, United Kingdom.

Lakonishok, J., Shleifer, A., and Vishny, R.W. (1992). The Impact of Institutional Trading on Stock Prices. Journal of Financial Economics 32 (1).

Leaton, J. (2014). Gone fishing: divestment and engagement. An article published by Carbon tracker, UK.

McKinsey & Company. (2021). How to develop a growth mindset. https://www.mckinsey.com/featured-insights/themes/how-to-develop-a-growth-mindset.

Meadows, D.H., Jørgen R., and Meadows, D.L. (2004). The Limits to Growth. Chelsea Green Publishing Company.

Meadows, D.H. (2008). Thinking in Systems: A Primer. White River Junction: Chelsea Green Publishing.

Meier, J. D., & Kropp, M. (2010). Getting Results the Agile Way: A Personal Results System for Work and Life. Bellevue, WA: Innovation Playhouse.

Miles, D. (1993). Testing for Short Termism in the UK Stock Market. The Economic Journal, 103(421), 1379–1396. https://doi.org/10.2307/2234472.

Ng, B. (2018). The Neuroscience of Growth Mindset and Intrinsic Motivation. Brain Sciences 8, no. 2: 20. https://doi.org/10.3390/brainsci8020020

Nickell, Stephen & Wadhwani, Sushil B. (1987). "Myopia, the 'Dividend Puzzle', and Share Prices," CEPR Discussion Papers 155, C.E.P.R. Discussion Papers.

Nidumolu, R., Prahalad, C.K., and Rangaswami, M.R. (2009). Why Sustainability Is Now the Key Driver of Innovation. An article published by Harvard Business Review.

Nofsinger, J.R. and Sias, R.W. (1999), Herding and Feedback Trading by Institutional and Individual Investors. The Journal of Finance, 54: 2263-2295. https://doi.org/10.1111/0022-1082.00188.

Norton Rose Fulbright. (2022). UK Pensions Briefing: Where are we now on ESG and Climate Change?

OECD. (2020). Beyond Growth: Towards a New Economic Approach, New Approaches to Economic Challenges, OECD Publishing, Paris, https://doi.org/10.1787/33a25ba3-en.

Piketty, T. (2013). Capital in the Twenty-First Century. Harvard University Press.

Primeau, M. (2021). Your powerful, changeable mindset. Stanford Report, Stanford University. https://news.stanford.edu/report/2021/09/15/mindsets-clearing-lens-life/

Principles for Responsible Investment. (2019). Fiduciary Duty in the 21st Century. https://www.unpri.org/download?ac=9792.

Principles for Responsible Investment.. (2016). Example investment beliefs. An article published by the PRI.

Reinecke, J., Arnold, D., & Palazzo, G. (2016). Qualitative Methods in Business Ethics, Corporate Responsibility, and Sustainability Research. Business Ethics Quarterly, 26(4), Xiii-Xxii. doi:10.1017/beq.2016.67

Richmond, B. (2000). The thinking in systems thinking: Seven essential skills. Waltham, MA: Pegasus Communications Inc.

Rimanoczy, I. (2022). Sustainability - We Need to Talk. Independently Published.

Rimanoczy, I. (2020). The Sustainability Mindset Principles: A Guide to Developing a Mindset for a Better World. The Principles for Responsible Management Education Series.

Rimanoczy, I. (2010). Business leaders committing to and fostering sustainability initiatives. New York, NY: Teachers College, Columbia University.

Schultz, S. (2004). Brain battles itself over short-term rewards, long-term goals. An article published by Princeton University. http://pr.princeton.edu/news/04/q4/1014-brain.htm.

Seligman, M. E., & Maier, S. F. (1967). Failure to escape traumatic shock. Journal of Experimental Psychology, 74(1), 1–9. https://doi.org/10.1037/h0024514.

Sharot, Tali. (2017). The Influential Mind: What the Brain Reveals About Our Power to Change Others. New York: Henry Holt and Company.

Shefrin, H., & Statman, M. (1994). Behavioral Capital Asset Pricing Theory. The Journal of Financial and Quantitative Analysis, 29(3), 323–349. https://doi.org/10.2307/2331334.

Shiller, R.J. (2000). Irrational Exuberance. Princeton: Princeton University Press.

Shleifer, A. and Vishny, R.W. (1990). Equilibrium short horizons of investors and firms. The American Economic Review, 80(2), pp.148-153.

Simon, H. A. (1982). Models of bounded rationality. Cambridge, MA: MIT Press. Rationality is bounded because there are limits to our thinking capacity, available information, and time.

Sinek, S. (2019). Start with why: How great leaders inspire everyone to take action. London: Portfolio/Penguin.

Smith, J. (2020). Growth Mindset vs Fixed Mindset: How what you think affects what you achieve. Published by mindset health.

Stein, J. (1989). Efficient capital markets, inefficient firms: A model of myopic corporate behaviour. Quarterly Journal of Economics, Vol.104(4):655-659.

Stiglitz, J. (2012). The Price of Inequality, Penguin.

Stiglitz, J. (2016). Inequality and economic growth. In Jacobs, M. and Mazzucato, M. (eds.) Rethinking Capitalism: Economics and Policy for Sustainable and Inclusive Growth. Wiley Blackwell.

Task Force on Climate-related Financial Disclosures. (2017). Final Report: Recommendations of the Task Force on Climate-related Financial Disclosures. https://www.fsb-tcfd.org/publications/final-recommendations-report/.

Thinking Ahead Institute. (2020). System thinking and investment: introducing the ecosystem perspective. A report published by Willis Towers Watson, UK.

Thinking Ahead Institute. (2017). Sustainability beliefs: A new measurement tool. A paper published by Willis Towers Watson, UK.

Tversky, A., & Kahneman, D. (1974). Judgment under uncertainty: Heuristics and biases. Science, 185(4157), 1124–1131. https://doi.org/10.1126/science.185.4157.1124.

UNEPFI. (2020). Financing Circularity: Demystifying Finance for the Circular Economy.

Victor P. (2019). Managing Without Growth: Slower by Design, Not Disaster. Edward Elgar, 2nd edition.

Waddock, S. (2010). Finding Wisdom Within - The Role of Seeing and Reflective Practice in Developing Moral Imagination, Aesthetic Sensibility, and Systems Understanding. Journal of Business Ethics Education; Edinburgh Vol. 7: 177-200.

Wahl, D.C. (2016). Designing Regenerative Cultures. Triarchy Press, Axminster, England.

Wahlquist, C. (2020). Rio Tinto blames misunderstanding for destruction of 46,000-year-old Aboriginal site. An article published by the Guardian.

Wahlquist, C. (2020). Rio Tinto blasts 46,000-year-old Aboriginal site to expand iron ore mine. An article published by the Guardian.

Watts, J. (2021). Oil firm bosses' pay incentivises them to undermine climate action. An article published by the Guardian.

WBCSD. (2020). Reinventing Capitalism: A Transformation Agenda. A report published by Volans and the World Business Council for Sustainable Development.

Weiner, B., & Kukla, A. (1970). An attributional analysis of achievement motivation. Journal of Personality and Social Psychology, 15(1), 1–20. https://doi.org/10.1037/h0029211

Wermers, R. (1999), Mutual Fund Herding and the Impact on Stock Prices. The Journal of Finance, 54: 581-622. https://doi.org/10.1111/0022-1082.00118.

Wolfe, I. (2022). Five Business Benefits Of Growth Mindset: How To Thrive In Today's Competitive Environment. An article published by Forbes.

Woolley, K., and Fishbach, A. (2017). Immediate Rewards Predict Adherence to Long-Term Goals. Personality and Social Psychology Bulletin, 43(2), 151–162. https://doi.org/10.1177/0146167216676480.

3. The need for capital allocation to combat climate change

"There's no shortage of money globally: it is simply that it has yet to travel to where it's most needed."
Source: IPCC (2023:1603)

"Financial institutions should focus not only on reducing their financed emissions, but also on financing emissions reduction… with deliberate and ambitious action, alongside government and real-economy efforts, the financial sector can help enable a global transition to net zero that helps avoid the worst impacts of climate change, minimizes firm-specific transition risks and stranded assets as well as broader risks to financial stability, and is just and orderly across countries and communities."
Source: GFANZ (2022:8)

We have now reviewed the broader purpose and role that the financial sector plays in how our society and economy functions and introduced the theoretical foundations for cultivating a sustainable mindset in finance. This chapter turns to examine the role that the finance sector could play in allocating capital to climate finance, to close the financing gap and help combat climate change.

Climate finance gap

Achieving the objective agreed in the Paris Agreement to limit global temperature increases to well below 2°C and pursuing efforts to limit it to 1.5°C from pre-industrial levels requires a whole economy transition—every company, bank, insurer, and investor will have to adjust their business models, develop credible plans for the transition and implement them (Carney, 2020). Achieving climate goals require all forms of finance, with the UNFCCC Cop27 Finance Day featuring the role of the finance sector as a core part of the solution to combat climate change (Carney, 2022).

Climate finance refers to local, national, or transnational financing—from public, private and alternative sources—that supports mitigation and adaptation actions that will address climate change (UNFCCC, n.d.). Climate finance is needed for mitigation because large-scale investments are required to significantly reduce emissions. Climate finance is equally important for adaptation, as significant financial resources are needed to adapt to the adverse effects and reduce the impacts of a changing climate.

A financing gap is defined as the difference between current flows and average needs to meet the long-term goals of the Paris Agreement (IPCC, 2023). Estimates of the financing gap are updated regularly as new data and evidence emerges. For the purposes of this review, the latest published estimates of the financing gap are as follows:

- **Mitigation financing gap:** To achieve net zero emissions by 2050, average annual investment in climate mitigation activities needs to increase to at least US$4 trillion per year by 2030, an increase from less than US$1 trillion per year in 2022 (IEA, 2022).
    - Estimates indicate that private sources need to contribute around three quarters of the investment needed by 2030 in the NZE Scenario, an over threefold increase from current levels (according to the IEA, 2022).

- **Adaptation financing gap:** Annual climate adaptation investment needs in developing countries are estimated in the range of US$160–340 billion by 2030 and US$315–565 billion by 2050 (UNEP, 2022), with the reported actual global public finance flows at $US28 billion in 2020 (IPCC, 2023). Based on this assessment, estimated adaptation needs are currently between five and 10 times higher than international adaptation finance flows, and the adaptation finance gap continues to widen.
  - Broader studies of the infrastructure investment needed estimate that $US 6.9 trillion a year to 2030 is required to meet climate and development objectives, with an estimated investment gap of $US2.5-3 trillion per annum (OECD, World Bank and UNEP (2018).
  - Most of the adaptation needs are currently financed by the public sector, with very little contribution by the private sector.

Institutional investors and climate finance

Institutional investors include pension funds, asset managers, superannuation funds, insurance companies, endowments and charities, and collectively manage in excess of USD $100 trillion of assets in the OECD countries, which is approximately 45% of the global capital markets as at end 2022 (OECD, various). Estimates indicate that less than 1% of institutional AUM in 2021 within the OECD countries was allocated to climate mitigation and adaptation activities (Climate Policy Initiative, 2022), which is very low and not proportionate to the concern and commitment that institutional investors have expressed about the systemic risks of climate change. Institutional investors could thus play a pivotal role in closing the climate financing gap by increasing their capital allocation to climate mitigation and adaptation activities as a high priority (BloombergNEF, 2022).

As the OECD (2021) observed and has been arguing for some time now, institutional investors are a natural fit to help finance the transition and resilience to climate change, as they not only have a large pool of capital available to invest, but they also have a long-term time horizon that sees them often described as patient capital, or long-term investors. This is not always the case as extreme market conditions and liquidity needs may require shorter time horizons from time to time, but in large part, institutional investors will have a longer time horizon than other private sector investors, such as corporations, commercial finance institutions or households/individuals. There are also domestic regulations in different jurisdictions that may limit investments into some markets and types of assets. Nevertheless, the role of institutional investors in financing the climate transition warrants further attention given their strong commitment to combat climate change, and the substantial pool of capital that they have available.

It is acknowledged that institutional investors can and do exercise their influence in a myriad of ways as part of addressing climate change, including through proxy resolutions and engagement with companies that they invest in to accelerate the climate transition, engaging with policy makers to encourage greater clarity and incentives to transition and adapt to climate change (UNEPFI, 2022), divestment from high carbon / climate damaging activities (Carbon Tracker, 2011) and through investing capital in climate-related solutions – the focus of this book.

The focus on climate change financing in this chapter does not imply that other sustainability challenges such as human rights, child labour, poverty alleviation or biodiversity (for example) are of any less importance, as sustainable outcomes require a holistic rethink at the systemic level. Indeed, the IPCC's Summary for Policymakers contribution to the Sixth Assessment Report explicitly recognised the interdependence of climate, ecosystems and biodiversity, and human societies and integrates knowledge more strongly across the natural, ecological, social and economic sciences than earlier IPCC assessments.

> The aim of focusing on a specific set of actors and a specific gap that needs to be filled is to develop a pathway for action that can be readily implemented, immediately. The decision to allocate capital to climate finance activities does not rely entirely on government policies, regulations or corporate disclosure. With a change in mindset, private sector investors have the potential to dramatically increase their allocation to activities that will help to mitigate the effects of climate change.

The climate transition financing gap

> According to the International Energy Agency, the investment flows that have been witnessed to date away from high carbon assets and towards lower carbon assets are minor compared to the massive shifts that are required to support a Net Zero by 2050 outcome. The decade that we are in now is the period when those flows need to be realised.

While there are a number of future scenarios that explore the financial flows that are needed to achieve Net Zero by 2050, one of the most pre-eminent sources on the future of the energy markets is the International Energy Agency's (IEA) Net Zero by 2050 scenario. The IEA's World Energy Outlook 2022 outlined the annual energy sector investment needed to achieve net zero by 2050.

The IEA's Net Zero by 2050 Scenario sets out a significant increase in investment into low emissions power supply, generation, infrastructure and end-use (in the industries, buildings and transport sectors) from less than $1 trillion currently, to over $4 trillion per year by 2030 (Figure 10). While the IEA pathways are focused on modelling the energy sector transition investment outlook, it also considers the additional investment required beyond clean energy, including land use, biodiversity, waste recycling, reduction and management and changing lifestyle and consumption patterns.

Figure 10. Global average annual investment to achieve Net Zero by 2050 (bn US$)

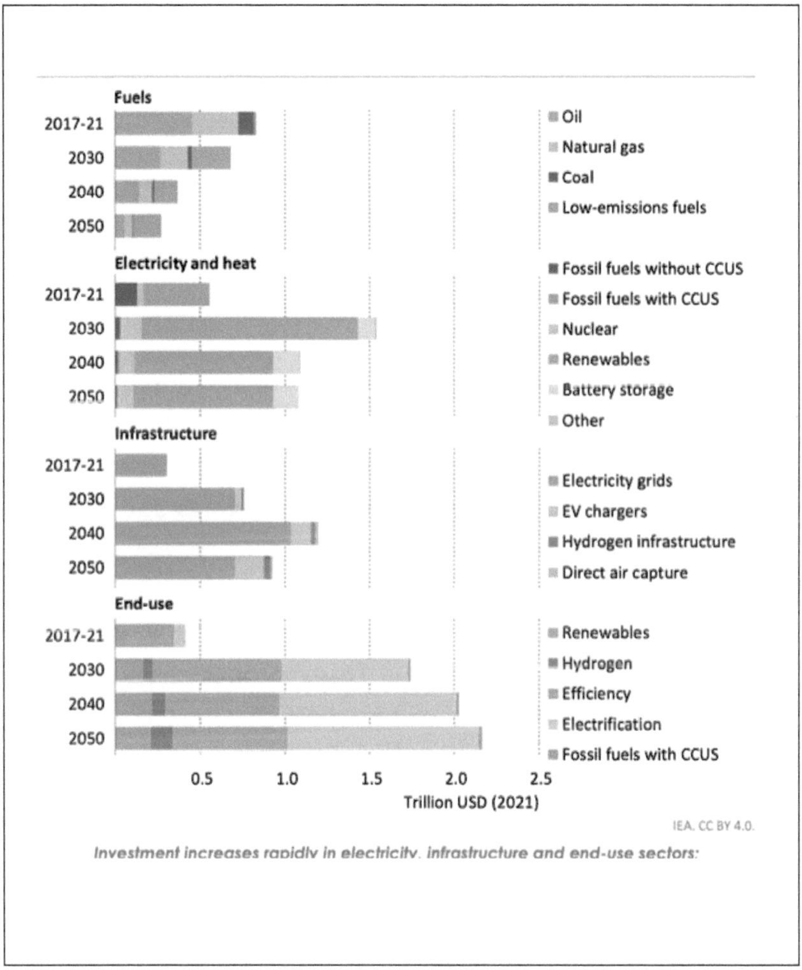

Source: IEA WEO 2022, page 163

A few notable observations from the IEA's WEO 2022 investment needs to achieve net zero by 2050 include:

- Investment in low-emissions fuels, including biofuels, low-emissions hydrogen and hydrogen-based fuels, increases from its current level of USD 18 billion to USD 235 billion in 2030. By 2050, low-emissions fuels account for over 65% of total investment in fuels, up from 1% in recent years.
- Investment in electricity and infrastructure more than doubles, while investment in end-use sectors increase more than fourfold to 2030 in the NZE Scenario.
- Electricity generation from renewables sees one of the largest increases, rising from USD 390 billion today to around USD 1 300 billion by 2030.
- To support the increase in renewables deployment, spending on electricity grids increases from USD 320 billion today to just over USD 740 billion in 2030.
- Spending on renewables for use in buildings and industry increases nearly threefold to 2030.
- Reaching net zero emissions requires an unprecedented acceleration in efficiency improvements and a significant reduction in energy intensity. This can be achieved through the rapid electrification of transport, heating, cooling and industrial production and a massive wave of retrofits and spending on new energy-efficient buildings. As a result, the share of investment directed to energy efficiency and electrification moves from 17% of the total today to 32% in 2030 and 40% in 2050.

The public/private sector financing breakdown

The IEA noted in its WEO 2022 analysis, the overall scale of investment required to get to a net zero emissions energy system is well beyond the capacity of governments to mobilise directly.

Over the course of the current decade, private sector investment in key elements of energy transitions needs to at least triple to get on track for net zero emissions by 2050 (Figure 11). A few observations of note:

- Private sources need to contribute around three quarters of the investment needed by 2030 in the NZE Scenario (an over threefold increase from current levels).
- Public spending is expected to rise, by slightly less than USD 800 billion from recent levels by 2030. This is primarily needed to boost the development of new infrastructure projects, accelerate innovation in technologies that are in the demonstration or prototype phase today, and provide de-risking measures that mobilise private capital and reduce financing costs.

Figure 11. Sources of finance to close the gap to Net Zero by 2050

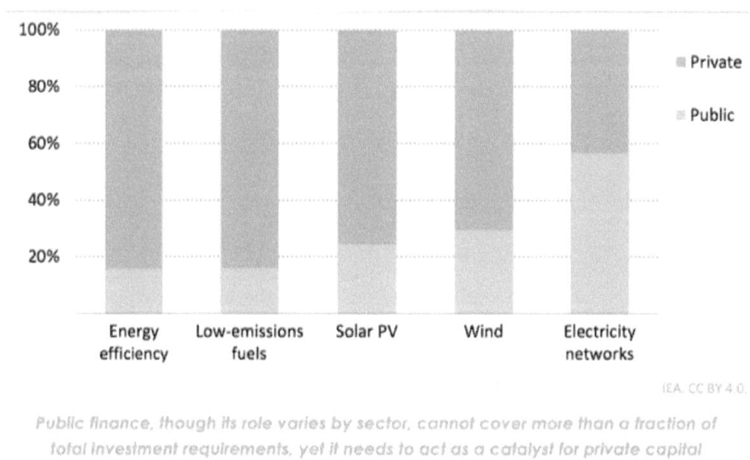

Source: IEA (2022:231)

Emerging versus developing economies transition financing needs

The OECD estimates that 70% of the $4 trillion of investment required for the energy transition will need to be in developing countries (Climate Finance Leadership Initiative, 2023). Despite this need, the current level of private sector clean energy investment is lower in emerging market / developing economies than it is in advanced economies. As a result, clean energy investment in emerging market and developing economies need to see a fourfold increase by 2030 in the NZE Scenario, compared with a less than threefold increase in advanced economies (Figure 12).

Figure 12. Net Zero by 2050 investment needs in advanced and emerging economies

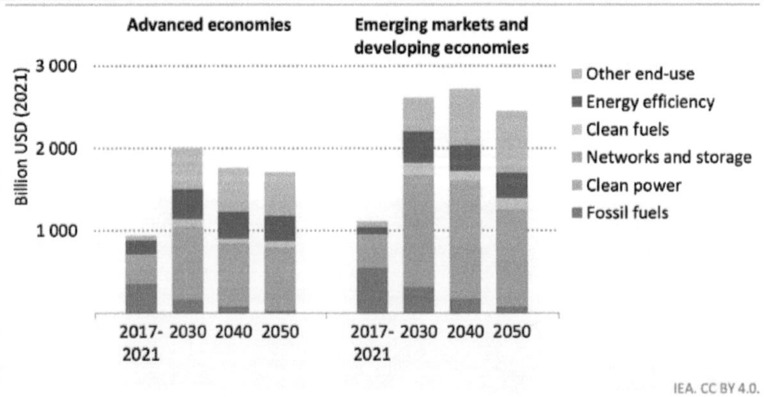

Clean energy investment increases four-times in emerging market and developing economies by 2030 and less than three-times in advanced economies

Note: Other end-use includes investment in electrification and direct use of renewables or low-emissions technologies in end-use sectors.

Source: IEA (2022:165)

The Glasgow Financial Alliance for Net Zero (GFANZ) has undertaken work to increase international flows to emerging markets and developing economies as a pillar of its workstream. GFANZ noted that:

> *"Creating investment-friendly business environments and strong pipelines of bankable net zero-aligned projects requires an approach tailored to each country and sector, as each market has its own diverse economic, legal, political, and financial circumstances."*
> Source: BloombergNEF (2022:6)

The approach GFANZ (2023) is taking is to provide bottom-up support to countries, donors, and multilaterals to explore and expand targeted, country-level public-private collaboration to leverage public sector finance and to help mobilize private capital. The network represents a large potential asset base of some over $100 trillion of AUM, although the members have not explicitly committed to allocate capital to climate finance, rather they are encouraging further collaboration and knowledge sharing to potentially enable and unblock some of the perceived barriers to climate finance flows.

> The barriers to climate finance are further considered in Chapters 5 and 6. This includes a discussion of the barriers to capital allocation that are most commonly cited, distinguishing between barriers that impact on the external conditions for the finance sector (e.g. regulations, policies, standards, guidelines, industry norms, tools, data and information), and those that are most relevant to the internal workings of the financial institutions themselves and the people who make the capital allocation decisions (e.g. mental models, assumptions, beliefs, biases, and worldview, to name a few). The GFANZ and other investor initiatives primarily focus their attention on the external barriers, with the internal barriers to climate financing remaining largely unexplored.

The climate adaptation financing gap

Climate change and extreme weather events are impacting on agriculture and food supply, infrastructure, precipitation, and water supply in ways that are only partially understood. This places lives, biodiversity, infrastructure, business models and assets at risk, and produces new opportunities in adaptation solutions and climate resilient infrastructure. The IPCC (2023) noted that these risks and impacts will intensify with each tenth of a degree, which means that investment in climate adaptation must take centre stage alongside mitigation in the global response to climate change.

The financing of climate adaptation refers to finance for actions to that help communities reduce the risks that they face and the harm that they might suffer from climate hazards, with a particular focus on the more vulnerable communities and regions of the world that are highly exposed to climate impacts and have less capacity to adapt to its effects. Adaptation finance includes public sector finance from developed to developing countries (via the Copenhagen Accord whereby developed countries committed to collectively mobilise US $100 billion per annum in climate finance to support developing countries in reducing emissions and adapting to climate change), as well as finance that governments — both developing and developed — invest towards meeting the costs of climate change damages and losses within their own borders (WRI:2022).

Adaptation finance also comes from private sources, although the finance sector has focused most of its attention on mitigation rather than adaptation actions. This is perhaps due to a belief within the financial sector that the impacts might be a long way into the future; the uncertainty of generating a sufficient investment return on the expenditure; and/or the assumption that a policy or technological solution might emerge in time to avoid large-scale climate change impacts from occurring.

However, in the face of the effects of climate change that we are already experiencing today in the form of severe floods, long-term droughts, worsening forest fires and biodiversity loss, there is a growing realisation from within the finance sector that it also needs to finance adaptation activities. Building resilience to the effects of climate change is vital to underpin the efficient functioning of the financial system and the ability for the sector to adequately serve the needs of its stakeholders and end beneficiaries. Clearly a world in turmoil due to climate hazards is not in anyone's best interests.

Songwe, Stern and Bhattacharya (2022) noted that there is significant potential for private sector finance to increase, particularly given the fiscal constraints that many governments around the world are under. It was also noted that whilst momentum is growing among mainstream investors, the level of private finance being mobilised today is *"far too little and will have to increase many times over"* (2022:9). The Bank of America estimated that the climate adaptation market could be worth $2 trillion a year within the next five years (Randall et al, 2023).

The gap between what we need to spend to adapt to climate change and what we are spending is widening. The UN (2022) estimated annual adaptation needs in developing countries in the range of US$160–340 billion per annum by 2030 and US$315–565 billion per annum by 2050. Against this, the reported actual global public finance flows for adaptation in 2020 were estimated at $US28 billion in 2020 (IPCC, 2023). Based on this assessment, estimated adaptation needs are currently between five and 10 times higher than international adaptation finance flows, and the adaptation finance gap continues to widen.

There are broader estimates of the financing needs to rebuild the world's essential infrastructure services in view of climate change. The OECD, World Bank and UNEP (2018) estimated that $US 6.9 trillion per annum to 2030 is required in infrastructure spending to meet climate and development objectives, with an estimated investment gap of $US2.5-3 trillion per annum. Around two-thirds of the required infrastructure investments are expected to take place in developing and emerging economies. With public budgets constrained in the aftermath of COVID-19, higher inflation and economic slowdown, partnerships and co-investment are needed between the public and private sector.

How much institutional investors contribute to climate financing

Building on the IEA's NZE2050 climate transition financing needs and the climate resilience gap, The Climate Policy Initiative (2021) identified the different sources of finance for climate mitigation and adaptation activities. This is particularly helpful when considering how much institutional investors are currently contributing to climate finance, compared to other sources of private finance.

The full data set is updated periodically and is open source. A summary of the key aspects of the data is provided in Figure 13.

Figure 13. Source of climate financing (mitigation and adaptation)

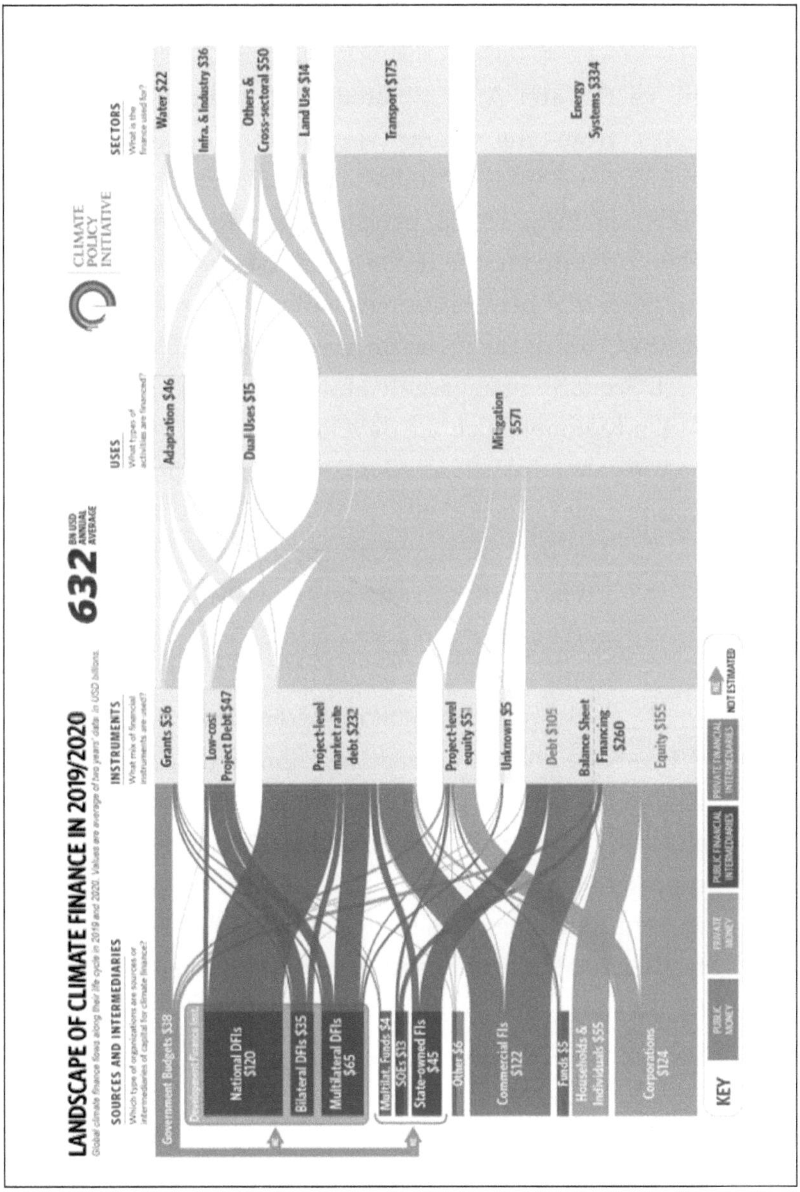

Source: CPI (2021)

Some of the key insights of the data in relation to institutional investors' contribution to the climate financing gap include:

- **Public vs Private:** An estimated 46% of finance currently emanates from the public sector and related agencies (including development banks and state-owned enterprises), with the remaining 55% of private sector financing.
    - This compared to the IEA's NZE2050 pathway which suggests that private sources will need to contribute around 75% of the investment needed by 2030 in the NZE Scenario in aggregate at the global level.
    - At the regional level, the developing and emerging regions are currently predominantly financed by the public sector (around 60% public, 40% private).
        - The IEA net zero pathway suggests this will pivot to 60% private capital in the developing and emerging regions, and 85% private capital in the developed world (averaging to 75% private financing at the global level).
    - While State Owned enterprises represent approximately 15% of the emerging regions source of finance currently, the development banks and institutions represent a much larger portion at around 35% of current financing. This makes partnerships between institutional investors and development institutions (at the multilateral and national level) essential for closing the financing gap to net zero by 2050.

- **Type of financing instrument:** The primary financing instrument used by commercial institutions are balance sheet debt financing and project-level debt, whereas for corporations the primary financing instruments are balance sheet equity financing and project-level equity.

- In contrast, for institutional investors the dominant financing instrument used is project-level equity and debt (green bonds), with some balance sheet financing albeit a much small proportion.

- **Type of private sector financier:** Private sector financing is currently dominated by commercial financial institutions (commercial and investment banks) and corporations, contributing 78% of the private sector financing of climate mitigation and adaptation investments in 2019/20 (CPI, 2021).
  - In contrast, investment funds and institutional investors combined only represent 3% of the private sector's financing of climate mitigation activities.
  - While there is some indirect exposure through the ownership of the banks and corporations that invest in such activities (secondary exposure), the current level of discrete financing of climate mitigation activities by the institutional investment community is extremely low.

Figure 14. Climate financing average annual needs to achieve Net Zero by 2050

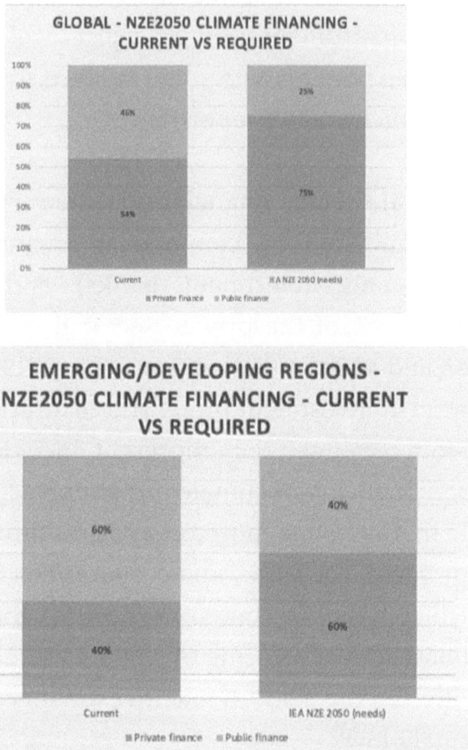

Source: Estimates based on Climate Policy Initiative (2021)

To put these figures into context, Figure 15 illustrates the current proportion of climate financing for each type of private sector agent, compared to available capital. Institutional investors represent the largest pool of capital within the private sector, yet their combined contribution to average annual investment flows into climate finance (including mitigation and adaptation

financing) is miniscule compare to their asset base (at 0.01%). Commercial financial institutions
and corporations currently make up the majority of private sector investments in climate finance to date, although their share was also still low at less than 2% pa of available capital.

Figure 15. Private sector climate financing activities versus available capital

Type of private sector financier	Proportion of TOTAL climate financing*	Proportion of PRIVATE SECTOR climate financing*	Average annual climate finance ($US) billion (pa)**	Pool of capital ($US) billion^, 2021	% available capital (pa)
Commercial Financial Institutions (loan book)	19%	38%	122	9,700	1.3%
Corporations (capex)	19%	39%	125	7,900	1.6%
Institutional investors (asset base)	1%	3%	9.5	104,400	0.01%

Source: Calculated by Climate Insight based on the IEA's NZE2050 scenario and the Climate Policy Initiative financing data. Institutional investors include investment funds, pension funds, insurance companies, public / reserve funds, endowments and charities.

* Based on Climate Policy Initiative data, 2021, Mitigation + Adaptation. Other private sector intermediaries include Households/Individuals
** Where data refers to the average annual investment data as reported by Climate Policy Initiative in 2021, 2019/2020 average
^ Where the pool of capital in 2021 for Commercial Financial Institutions refers to the size of the global commercial lending market (https://www.researchdive.com/8579/commercial-lending-market); Corporations refers to

the size of global capital expenditure (https://www.spglobal.com/_assets/documents/ratings/research/100288873.pdf) and Funds / Institutional Investors refer to the size of assets under management (https://www.thinkingaheadinstitute.org/news/article/global-asset-manager-aum-tops-us100-trillion-for-the-first-time/)

> Despite hundreds of financial institutions with trillions of dollars of assets under management having committed to support the attainment of Net Zero by 2050 and climate resilience, the capital allocation to climate financing activities remains extremely low as a proportion of the capital that is available.

Why climate change is relevant for capital allocation decisions

> Institutional investors could play an important role in closing the climate finance gap through their capital allocation decisions. Such investments not only provide the potential advantage of improving risk adjusted returns through improved portfolio diversification and risk mitigation, but they will also help to mitigate and adapt to climate change across the real economy, thus serving the broader needs of end beneficiaries and stakeholders by supporting greater social cohesion and resilience.

It is widely recognised that the long-term capital allocation decisions are the most important investment decisions for investors to make to fulfill their fiduciary duty and manage the variability in portfolio performance over the long term (Brinson et al, 1991). At the same time, many institutional investors have committed to incorporate climate change into investment processes, which has implications not only at the asset and stock level, but also for how

exposures aggregate up and impact on the resilience at the total portfolio level. However, the allocation of capital to finance the mitigation and adaption needs has been nascent up to now.
We have seen the potential benefits of capital allocation to climate finance in terms of supporting a more stable, secure, and resilient future for all. But often investors get stuck at the point of analysing the specific portfolio implications of making such decisions and fail to see the bigger picture and their role in not only aligning with net zero and climate resilience but taking the important next step – allocating capital to *enable* that outcome.

There can be a quest for perfect information and certainty, in a world where those conditions do not exist on any investment issue, let alone climate change. While there is no historical precedence to analyse the portfolio impacts of investing in climate mitigation and adaptation opportunities, there are certainly credible and robust tools (such as scenario analysis) that are available to support such decisions. There is evidence to suggest that such a strategy would be beneficial for portfolio performance in terms of reduced risk and higher performance (Cheema-Fox, Serafeim and Wang, 2022, IPR, 2021, Mercer, 2011; 2015).

So, the implications are clear. Institutional investors need to explicitly incorporate a goal to allocate capital into climate mitigation and adaptation activities to enable the attainment of net zero by 2050 and to build climate resilience, with a level of urgency and priority that the climate crisis necessitates.

An important distinction to consider is whether investors have committed to align their portfolios with a net zero by 2050 pathway, or they have committed to help achieve that outcome. By investing to enable net zero, investors become an active part of the solution, which requires additional investment and capital allocation to support the climate-related transition and resilience solutions beyond the levels that we are seeing today.

What does this mean in practice? Box 2 summarises ways in which climate change relates to capital allocation decision-making processes.

Box 2. Capital allocation decisions and climate change

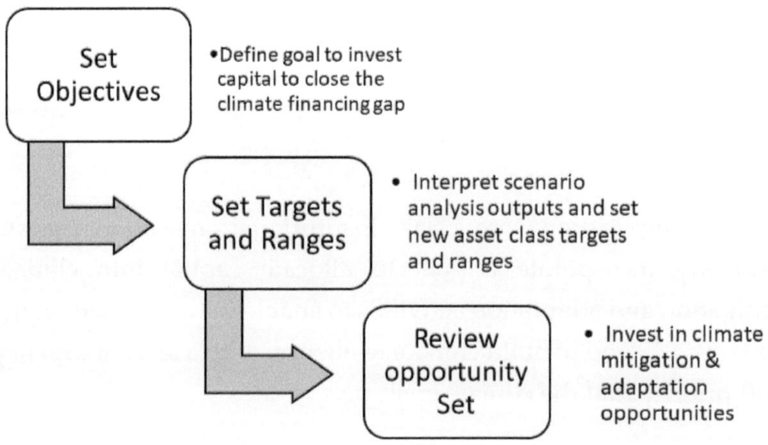

Source: Adapted from PRI (2019)

While the approach to capital allocation varies across different types of investors, the most traditional approach builds on Mean-Variance Optimisation (MVO), which is well known to have its limitations not least given its heavy reliance on historical data and relationships that might not prove to be robust or reliable in the future (Michaud, 2004). While some of optimisation techniques and models have made improvements to the more standard MVO approach, as highlighted in Figure 16, most investors still utilise some form of optimisation in terms of the end-outputs to guide capital allocation decisions.

Figure 16. Climate change and capital allocation approaches

Model	Features	Potential link to climate change	Outputs to reflect climate change
Mean-variance optimization (MVO) Markowitz, 1952; Black & Litterman, 1991	MVO results in the construction of an efficient frontier that represents a mix of assets that produces the minimum standard deviation (as a proxy for risk) for the maximum level of expected return. It is based on defined asset class buckets and long-term expected returns, risk and correlations	MVO is highly sensitive to baseline assumptions, making it imperative to fully understand any revised assumptions due to climate change considerations. Highly dependent on historical data as the baseline with adjustments made to reflect future expectations. Volatility as a proxy for risk does not work well in cases of fat tail risk and large market swings	Climate change could impact on assumptions regarding expected return, volatility and correlation assumptions at the asset and sub asset class level. Climate change issues also have the potential to expand the regional and asset class mix and to add new sub asset classes to align with the pursuit of positive real-world impact

Factor risk allocation Idzorek et al, 2013	Factor risk frameworks seek to build a diversified portfolio based on sources of risk. Typically includes factors such as fundamental risks (GDP, interest rates, inflation) as well as market risks (equity risk premium, illiquidity, volatility)	The macroeconomic links to climate change issues are more difficult to quantify with precision from a purely top down perspective. Market risk factors can also be built from the bottom up using asset and sector level analysis	Climate change could require a change to baseline factor risk assumptions, potential to build in new 'climate-related' risk factors (such as climate change) to improve diversification (particularly across market risk factors)
Total Portfolio Analysis Thinking Ahead Institute, 2019	Similar to factor risk allocation, TPA allows for closer review and interplay between strategy setting process and alignment of investment goals. Based on an agreed risk budget, asset allocations are made on expected risk exposures and less constrained by asset class 'buckets' as traditional MVO approaches	TPA is relevant to consider climate change issues that require the interplay between judgement about the future, and quantitative analysis. TPA requires specialist knowledge to make informed judgements about future risk.	TPA's emphasis on risk budgeting and allocation of capital to opportunities within that budget (bringing alignment between top down and bottom up) would provide greater flexibility to capture the potential winners and losers in scenario analysis that also incorporate climate-related issues

Dynamic asset allocation Jarvis et al, 2012	DAA is driven by changes in risk tolerance, typically induced by cumulative performance relative to investment goals or an approaching investment horizon	DAA could introduce additional source of estimation errors due to need for dynamic rebalancing	DAA has the potential to reflect change in baseline assumptions over different time horizons
Liability driven asset allocation Hoevenaars et al, 2008	LDI seeks to find the most efficient asset class mix driven by a fund's liabilities. Simultaneously concerned with the return of the assets, the change in value of the liabilities, and how assets and liabilities interact to determine the overall portfolio value	LDI encounters the same limitations as MVO, with high sensitivity to baseline assumptions	Some climate change issues could potentially impact on inflation and alter liability assumptions

Regime Switching Models Ang & Timmerman, 2011	Regime switching approaches model abrupt and persistent changes in financial variables due to shifts in regulations, policies and other secular changes. Captures fat tails, skewness, and time-varying correlations	Regime switching approaches are relevant for considering climate change issues where an abrupt shift is expected over time. It is also typically based more on forward looking rather than historical data	These approaches have the potential to capture dramatic shifts in investment environment. Models not yet widely utilised by investment practitioners

Source: Updated and adapted from PRI (2018)

Summary

This chapter examined the investment gap that exists to achieve Net Zero by 2050 and what is needed to build climate resilience, the required split between public and private capital, and how the gap breaks down into different types of assets and regions. We have focused on institutional investors given the unique role that they play as long-term investors with a broad remit.

We have seen that the institutional investment community has a significant pool of capital available to invest compared to the other major private sector financiers, although it is financing the smallest share of discrete climate financing activities. We have also seen that there are potential benefits for increasing the financing of capital as it would help to enable a safer, more secure, and resilient future for all, that aligns with the industry's broader sense of purpose in serving the needs of its end beneficiaries and stakeholders.

Similarly, the benefits in terms of increased diversification, reduced risk, and higher potential returns from investing in climate solutions reaffirms the benefits of such activities.

While there are efforts underway to address this gap within the investment community via initiatives such as GFANZ, most of these efforts focus on the external conditions that prevail, rather than looking also at the internal barriers to action that might be slowing down progress.

> The data indicates that institutional investors' share of climate mitigation and adaptation financing has the potential to increase considerably from current levels, with expansion into developing and emerging markets and potential partnerships with development institutions being an essential part of the future financing strategy. Given the strong public position and commitment that many institutional investors have made regarding climate change, the question remains as to what barriers stand in the way for investors to allocate more capital to climate finance with the urgency that is required. We will now turn to examine some of these barriers – including the external and internal conditions - before moving on to explore how we might approach these perceived barriers differently, through shifting our mindset.

References

Ang, A., and Timmerman, A. (2011). Regime Changes and Financial Markets, NBER Working Paper No. 17182, http://www.nber.org/papers/w17182.

Black, F., and Litterman, R. (1991). Asset Allocation: Combing Investor Views with Market Equilibrium. Journal of Fixed Income, 1, 7-18.

Bloomberg NEF. (2022). Mobilizing Capital into Emerging Markets and Developing Economies. Commissioned by GFANZ. Published by BloombergNEF. Available at: https://assets.bbhub.io/professional/sites/24/Mobilizing-Capital-to-EMDEs.pdf.

Brinson, G.P., Singer, B.D., and Beebower, G.L. (1991). Determinants of Portfolio Performance II: An Update, Financial Analysts Journal, May/June 1991, 47, 3; Ibbotson and Kaplan 2000; Xiong, Ibbotson, Idzorek and Chen, 2010.

Carbon Tracker. (2011). Unburnable Carbon: are the world's financial markets carrying a carbon bubble? https://carbontracker.org/reports/carbon-bubble/

Carney, M. (2020). Building a financial system for net zero, Priorities for private finance for COP26. UN Special Envoy for Climate Action and Finance and the Prime Minister's Finance Adviser for COP26.

Carney, M. (2022). Climate Finance in a Polycrisis Era. A presentation to Cop27 Finance Day. https://assets.bbhub.io/company/sites/63/2022/11/COP27-Finance-Day-Opening-Keynote.pdf

Cheema-Fox, A. Serafeim, G., and Wang, H.S. (2022). Climate change solutions. Harvard Business School Working Paper 22-054. https://www.hbs.edu/ris/Publication%20Files/22-054_6cf2092f-aab9-4b37-90c0-9f33dd24b04a.pdf

Climate Finance Leadership Initiative. (2023). Financing sustainable infrastructure in emerging markets. https://www.bloomberg.com/cfli/mobilizing-investment/.

Climate Policy Initiative. (2021). Global Landscape of Climate Finance. https://www.climatepolicyinitiative.org/publication/global-landscape-of-climate-finance-2021/

Glasgow Financial Alliance for Net Zero. (2022). Financial institution net-zero transition plans: fundamentals, recommendations and guidance. Published by GFANZ. Available at: https://assets.bbhub.io/company/sites/63/2022/09/Recommendations-and-Guidance-on-Financial-Institution-Net-zero-Transition-Plans-November-2022.pdf.

Hoevenaars, P.M.M., Molenaar, R.D.J., Schotman, P.C., and Steenkamp, T.B.M. (2008). Strategic asset allocation with liabilities: Beyond stocks and bonds, Journal of Economic Dynamics and Control, Vol.32, Issue 9, pp. 2939-2970.

Idzorek, T.M and Kowara, M. (2013). Financial Analysts Journal, Vol. 69, Issue 3, Factor Based Asset Allocation vs. Asset Class-Based Asset Allocation

Intergovernmental Panel on Climate Change. (2023). AR6 Synthesis Report: Climate Change. https://www.ipcc.ch/report/sixth-assessment-report-cycle/.

International Energy Agency. (2022). World Energy Outlook 2022, Net Zero by 2050 scenario and investment needs. www.iea.org

IPR. (2021). The inevitable policy response to climate change, a program of work. Published by Capital Transition Monitor. https://ipr.transitionmonitor.com/2023-04-20-current-ipr-policy-scenario-forecasts/.

Jarvis, S., Lawrence, A., and Miao S. (2012). Dynamic Asset Allocation techniques, British Actuarial Journal, Vol.15, Issue 3, pp. 573-655.

Markowitz, H. (1952). Portfolio Selection. The Journal of Finance, Vol. 7, No. 1, pp. 77-91.

Mercer. (2015). Investing in a time of change. A report published by Mercer. Available at https://www.mercer.com.au/content/dam/mercer/attachments/asia-pacific/australia/investment/sustainable-growth/mercer-climate-change-study-2015.pdf.

Mercer. (2011). Climate Change Scenarios — Implications for Strategic Asset Allocation. Available at: http://www.mercer.com/content/dam/mercer/attachments/global/investments/responsible-investment/Climate-change-scenarios-Implications-for-strategic-asset-allocation.pdf

Michaud, R.O. (2004). Why Mean-Variance Optimization Isn't Useful for Investment Management. An article published by New Frontier Advisors.

OECD. (various). Global Pension Statistics, OECD Global Insurance Statistics and OECD Institutional Investors Statistics databases.

OECD. (2021). Mobilising institutional investors for financing sustainable development in developing countries: Emerging evidence of opportunities and challenges. An OECD publication. https://www.oecd.org/dac/financing-sustainable-development/Mobilising-institutional-investors-for-financing-sustainable-development-final.pdf

OECD, The World Bank and UN Environment Program. (2018). Financing Climate Futures: Rethinking Infrastructure. OECD Publishing, Paris, https://doi.org/10.1787/4d36800f-en.

PRI. (2019). Implications for strategic asset allocation. A paper published by the PRI as part of a program of work on the Inevitable Policy Response to climate change.

PRI. (2018). Asset owner strategy guide: How to craft an investment strategy. A paper published by the PRI as part of a program of work on integrating ESG factors into investment strategy.

Randall,T., Sedemund,J. and Bartz-Zuccala, W. (2023). Private investment for climate change adaptation – difficult to finance or difficult to see the finance? An article published by the LSE Grantham Research Institute.

Thinking Ahead Institute. (2019). Total Portfolio Approach. A global asset owner study into current and future asset allocation practices. An article published by Willis Towers Watson.

UNEP. (2022). Adaptation Gap Report 2022: Too little, too slow. A UNEP published research report.

UNEPFI. (2022). 500-plus institutional investors urge governments to step-up climate ambition. https://www.unepfi.org/industries/investment/500-plus-institutional-investors-urge-governments-to-step-up-climate-ambition/

UNFCCC. (n.d.) Introduction to climate finance. https://unfccc.int/topics/introduction-to-climate-finance

4. External barriers to climate financing

"Domestic and international private investment in green infrastructure is still seriously constrained by market failures and specific investment barriers."
OECD (2013:4)

"The cost-competitiveness of clean technologies in developing countries has historically been hampered by the fact that local financing costs can be higher than in wealthier nations….

…Other barriers include inconsistent clean energy procurement from state-run utilities, ineffective or non-existent transmission infrastructure planning, fossil fuel subsidies, non-creditworthy offtakers and currency risk."
BloombergNEF (2022:20)

While many investors recognise the growing need to incorporate climate change into investment decisions and have made public commitments to act on climate change, we have seen that the allocation of capital to mitigation and adaptation activities is very low, and the financing gap remains wide. It is of course noted that financial institutions can (and do) utilise their power and influence in other ways, such as engaging with governments, and companies that they are invested in to encourage greater climate action. However, it is evident from the climate financing data that the allocation of capital by financial institutions is insufficient and needs to increase considerably to build resilience and achieve the transition to net zero.

Figure 17 classifies the financing barriers into external and internal barriers, whereby:

- **External barriers** include factors that impact on the external conditions for financial institutions, such as data and information, industry standards, reporting standards, regulations, and government policies.
    - The majority of the policy discussions, investor guidance material, research and literature exploring the barriers to climate financing within the private sector tend to focus on external conditions, and how they might be overcome.

- **Internal barriers** refer to the internal conditions that influence decision-making processes and how people inside financial institutions interpret information, including their mental models, beliefs, values, assumptions and biases.
    - There is very little policy discussion, investor guidance, research or literature on the internal barriers to climate financing from the private sector, or how these might be managed.

- The external and internal barriers are inter-related, because how we describe external barriers will be influenced by how we see the world, how we make sense of the world, the assumptions we make and the industry norms that we adhere to (perhaps unknowingly). In that way, our internal dimensions also impact on our perception of the external barriers to climate financing.

Figure 17. External and internal barriers to climate finance

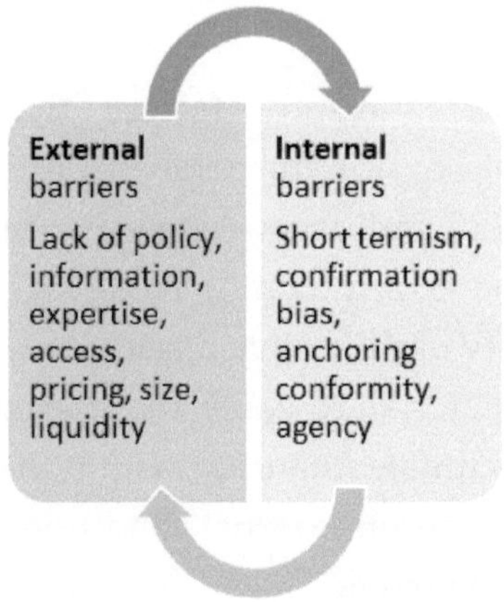

Source: Adapted from Guyatt, Poulter (2019)

This chapter explores some of the external barriers that are most commonly cited to explain why financial institutions are not allocating capital to climate mitigation and adaptation financing at the speed and scale required.

At the industry wide and regulatory level, proponents of investor action on climate change tend to focus their efforts on addressing these external conditions, such as government policies, regulatory guidance, developing best practice processes, improving data, tools and metrics in the hope that knowledge and information will propel investors into action. Indeed, this is the dominant narrative underpinning the FSB's TCFD recommendations and the efforts of the GFANZ network, as well as other investor networks such as the PRI, UNEP FI, IIGCC and IGCC, amongst others.[6]

This chapter examines the literature and evidence that underpin such explanations and responses. We will also unravel some of the assumptions that are embedded into these explanations and consider if there could be alternative explanations for the perceived barriers to capital allocation as they are currently presented. The aim is not to suggest that the external barriers are not valid or important, but rather to invite a wider conversation and set of actions that can look at how we consider these barriers with a broader lens. Given the scale and urgency of climate change, action and enquiry on all pillars is necessary.

Literature and evidence

The OECD, the PRI, various climate change investor groups and industry bodies have explored some of the barriers to climate financing over the past decade (PRI, 2022; OECD, 2013, 2015; IGCC, 2022; and BloombergNEF, 2020). The most widely cited explanations tend to fall into the following categories, all of which relate to the external environment in which financial institutions make their capital allocation decisions. These categories include (but are not limited to):

1. Inconsistent government policy
2. Lack of information
3. Lack of common definitions
4. Lack of expertise
5. Liquidity barriers
6. Excessive deal pricing
7. Difficulty to access

Let's explore each of these barriers further, focusing on how investors themselves describe and think about these obstacles. We will also consider an alternative perspective for each of the identified issues, to invite further enquiry into understanding these perceived challenges.

Inconsistent government policy

One of the most common explanations for the lack of capital allocation to climate finance from the perspective of the financial sector and institutional investors, is the prevailing inconsistency in government policies. This is the starting point for most interactions and dialogue between investors and governments.

A good example to illustrate this is The Investor Agenda (2022)[7] statement to G20 leaders that was signed by over 600 international investors with more than US$42 trillion of assets under management, evidently a large and powerful network that has the potential to make a significant dent in closing the climate financing gap. The network requested that governments:

- Fully implement the Paris Agreement to create investment opportunities in clean technologies, green infrastructure and other assets, products and services needed.
- Guarantee energy security by scaling up the deployment of low-carbon energy systems, electrification, flexibility and storage, including the development of enabling infrastructure (with a particular focus on emerging markets).
- Implement carbon pricing mechanisms.
- Set a deadline to phase out thermal coal power and remove fossil fuel subsidies.

According to the letter presented to government leaders (drafted by the financial sector) if these conditions were met then investors would be able to allocate more capital to climate finance, amongst other activities. In the meantime, the statement explains that investors will play an active stewardship role, by engaging with governments and companies to request change, the inference being that when the policy changes occur, they would also be able to allocate more capital to climate finance.

Investor groups have spent considerable time analysing government policy settings, describing the changes that they believe would allow them to invest in climate related activities at the scale and pace that is required. For example, a study led by the IGCC (2022), a network of investors in Australia, developed an array of published material and workshop contents that took extensive time and effort to produce, detailing quite considerably the actions that they would like governments to take to allow them to then play their role in climate financing. In addition to the requests directed to all international leaders, the further requests to domestic government included actions such as:

- Implement mandatory risk disclosure.
- Define sector goals and pathways.
- Create demand for green products.
- Remove barriers to investment in pre-commercial technologies.
- National coordination in climate adaptation activities.
- Upgrade building codes and land-use plans.

While engagement between investors and governments is a positive development and indeed, this wish list of actions expected of governments is extensive. There is no doubt that government policies need enhancement and ongoing refinement to tackle the critical risks that climate change presents. However, if the finance sector waits until all these policy requests are met, then the climate financing gap will remain wide for some time. This increases the risk that we will collectively fail to address the barriers in time to avoid catastrophic outcomes, as financing plays a critical role in enabling mitigation and adaptation activities.

Given how far we have come in the climate discussions and commitments through the UNFCCC COP process, the direction of travel is clear. This means that in many cases, government policy refinement is a 'nice to have' rather than essential for fundamental change, as we all know and understand what is needed. Requesting governments implement full and coherent policy settings is one thing but failing to allocate capital in lieu of these perfect settings is a high-risk strategy for investors to take. It is quite common for there to be inconsistencies in government policies on a range of issues (think of social welfare and taxation policies; global inequality and tax havens, for example); this need not be a reason for inaction on climate finance.

Investors have options and alternative ways to think about and approach these perceived barriers and to increase capital allocation within the emerging (and imperfect) policy context, as we will explore in Chapter 7 when we apply the mindset framework.

Lack of information

Another prominent explanation put forward by the finance sector as a barrier to climate finance is the lack of information. The information gap was indeed one of the founding principles for establishing the TCFD and the recommendations for reporting and disclosure that continue to follow on from that process. The TCFD concluded that more effective, clear, and consistent climate-related disclosure is needed from companies around the world. The recommendations focused on improving the quantity, quality, and comparability of climate-related disclosures, by developing a common framework for disclosure across all regions and sectors of the global economy.

The rationale put forward by the convening group behind the TCFD (which was represented by corporations, insurance companies, banks, asset managers and asset owners) included:

- Market function - one of the essential functions of financial markets is to price risk to support informed, efficient capital-allocation decisions. Without the right information about climate change, investors and others may incorrectly price or value assets, leading to a misallocation of capital.
- Complexity – the large-scale and complex nature of climate change makes it uniquely challenging, especially in the context of economic decision-making.
- Transparency – information is needed to help stakeholders to better understand the concentrations of carbon-related assets in the financial sector and the financial system's exposures to climate-related risks. Including regulators.
- Valuations – the concern that present asset valuations did not adequately factor in climate-related risks because of insufficient information.
- Investment decisions – the expectation that more information would promote more informed investment, credit, and insurance underwriting decisions.

In summing up, by improving disclosure and increasing transparency, the thinking behind the TCFD recommendations was that investors, lenders, and insurance underwriters would have adequate information on how companies are preparing for a lower carbon economy and be better equipped to value assets and make the investments needed.

Since the TCFD recommendations were initially released in 2017, there has been an ongoing process of review and adoption of the recommendations around the world, with the TCFD framework becoming the new standard for financial reporting on climate impacts by companies and financial institutions. This has been reinforced by financial regulators, financial standard setting bodies and central banks, and supported by governments in developed and emerging economies.

We are now (2023, at the time of writing this book) - 5 years on from the initial TCFD recommendations - so it is pertinent to consider if the information gap has closed at all in that time, and the visible impact that this additional information has had (if any) on capital allocation to climate mitigation and adaptation activities by the financial sector. The TCFD (2022) undertook an annual review of progress for 2022 which highlighted that:

- Disclosure has improved considerably.
  - For fiscal year 2021 reporting, 80% of companies disclosed in line with at least one of the 11 recommended disclosures.
  - The percent of companies disclosing the TCFD recommendations in financial filings or annual reports has increased with over 70% of companies implementing

the TCFD recommendations disclosed climate-related information in financial filings or annual reports for fiscal year 2021 (compared to 45% for fiscal year 2017).

- The availability and quality of climate-related financial disclosures has increased since June 2017.
  - Ninety-five percent (95%) of survey respondents saw an increase in the availability of climate-related financial disclosures since the release of the TCFD recommendations, with 88% of respondents citing improvements in the quality of disclosures.

- Investors and others use disclosures in decision-making and pricing.
  - Based on the TCFD survey, 90% of investors and other users incorporate climate-related financial disclosures in financial decision-making, and 66% of these indicated such disclosures factor into the way they price financial assets.
  - Over 615 investors with more than $60 trillion in assets under management committed to engage with the world's largest corporate greenhouse gas emitters to strengthen their climate-related disclosures by implementing the TCFD recommendations as part of Climate Action 100+.
  - Over 680 financial institutions with more than $130 trillion in assets have asked 10,000+ companies to disclose via CDP, which has aligned its questionnaires with the TCFD recommendations.
  - In addition, based on a literature review, there is a growing body of evidence that climate-related risks are beginning to affect prices for certain types of assets.

On the face of it, this appears to indicate that good progress has been made. Information availability on climate impacts has increased considerably, and it seems that investors are using this information to engage further with companies. However, there is no evidence that this has had any impact on valuations or capital allocation decisions. The best the TCFD could report is that *"climate-related risks are beginning to affect prices for certain types of assets"* (TCFD, 2022:5).

The industry identified lack of information as a barrier to climate finance, whereby more information would reportedly lead to better valuation frameworks and increased capital allocation. Yet the climate finance gap remains wide and the allocation of capital by institutional investors (as we saw in the preceding discussion) is miniscule in terms of their assets under management. The increased flow of information has not increased investor's capital allocation to climate finance.

We could argue that it is early days, perhaps there is a longer time lag needed before we will see progress. Perhaps the International Sustainability Standards Board (ISSB) climate-related disclosure standards will make a difference, although these standards do not go any further towards clarifying or establishing common definitions but rather reinforce the TCFD recommendations (ISSB, 2023). Is it possible that while the climate-related financial information has improved, there is something else that is holding investors back in terms of how they interpret that information and how it is used? In other words, it is not only the information that matters, but how people interpret and use that information.

We could search hard to find further justification for the apparent absence of a positive connection between increased climate-related financial information and capital allocation to climate finance. Or we could pause to reflect on what else might be happening and consider an alternative perspective, as we will do in Chapter 7 when we apply the mindset framework. Is it possible that investors are overlooking the most important and obvious information that is right in front of them? The science of climate change, the economic costs of climate change, the regions and sectors that will be impacted, the industries of the future, technological pathways, policy pathways. There is a plethora of data and research, robust evidence, on all of these issues from credible sources. Is the quest for more information an unintentional delay tactic, an avoidance strategy – or at best, an admission that there could be a need to build a deeper understanding of these issues?

Lack of common definitions

The next obstacle to capital allocation that the financial sector has spent a great deal of time trying to solve over recent years is the lack of common definitions when it comes to classifying what is a climate mitigation / adaptation activity. This closely relates to the TCFD quest for information, but in this case the policy makers, regulators, corporations, and financial sector are seeking clarity on how to define sustainable economic activities.

The most prominent of these efforts has been the development of a taxonomy on sustainability in the EU that commenced in 2017 and is ongoing, with other countries following suit with a similar quest to define and categorise activities in this way.

Some of the taxonomies are focused on narrowly defining 'green' assets, others have a broader sustainability focus. But invariably climate mitigation and adaptation activities are an important component of the 20+ taxonomies that exist or are under development. The rationale for such activities is various, with the EU (2023) and ASFI (2023) explaining that taxonomies:

- Provide a set of common definitions for sustainable economic activities, which can be used to define sustainable investments.
- Provide companies, investors, and policymakers with definitions for which economic activities can be considered environmentally sustainable.
- Provide confidence and assurance for investors.
- Enable comparability between Investment products and portfolios to help protect private investors from greenwashing.
- Help companies to become more transparent in disclosing their activities.
- Shift investments where they are most needed to support the achievement of climate, environmental and social objectives.

It is thus anticipated that a taxonomy would (inter alia) help to shift capital to where it is most needed, which would include closing the climate financing gap. This outcome sits alongside other objectives as set out, nevertheless, it is one of the often-cited reasons why a taxonomy or set of common definitions is needed.

This is a laudable goal and body of work, that has involved (and will continue to involve) thousands of human hours of meetings, negotiations, analysis, and dialogue across a variety of stakeholders in more than 20 different jurisdictions. The process itself has produced some very positive outcomes in terms of fostering collaboration across countries and regions, as each jurisdiction shares their insights and learnings in formulating a set of common definitions of this kind.

However, there are some red flags to consider regarding how much impact taxonomies and common definitions will have on capital flows into climate finance activities in the short window of time that we have remaining to address the climate crisis.

The first red flag is the time intensive and laborious process that is involved in negotiating a sustainability taxonomy and set of common definitions that can be applied within each jurisdiction. For example, the EU taxonomy took more than 3 years from when discussions commenced to publish the taxonomy regulation that set out the high-level goals and scope of developing a taxonomy (in 2020), and a further 2 years before a first delegated act of listed activities was published (in 2022). There were thousands of hours of meetings, analysis and research that went on in that time, and the negotiation process became quite heated on some topics (on the treatment of gas and nuclear as transition assets, in other jurisdictions there will be different sensitivities depending on the industry base of the country) (S&P Global, 2022).

What this means is that the dozen or so countries that are now just starting their journey to negotiate a taxonomy in their jurisdictions could agree and codify a taxonomy by 2025 at the earliest (if we optimistically assume that the process in other countries runs quicker than the EU, perhaps learning from the EU process). Given that one of the goals underpinning the taxonomy is to close the climate financing gap by 2030, that leaves a very short window of time for investors to escalate their capital allocation decisions (maximum of 5 years). It also runs the risk that investors might decide to wait until the taxonomies are agreed and published before prioritising the allocation of capital to climate finance, which would mean the taxonomy process brings the unintended consequence of delaying investment decisions that need to be addressed with urgency.

A second red flag is the lack of common definitions that are emerging across jurisdictions. The industry and policy makers started out with the goal to agree common definitions to allow for comparability and consistency, yet already we are seeing that each region and country is developing their own unique set of definitions, to reflect the local context and industries in their jurisdictions. This lack of common definition undermines the usefulness of taxonomies for capital allocation purposes, as it means that each company and asset will disclose its activities in alignment with the definitions that prevail in each of the jurisdictions that they operate in. In a globalised world, this will make it very difficult for investors (or any agent for that matter) to aggregate what this means in terms of transition and adaptation activities, which was one of the fundamental reasons for developing a taxonomy in the first place. It is for this reason that the EU established the International Platform on Sustainable Finance, of which one of its activities is to find common ground in the prevailing sustainable taxonomies between the EU and China. A summary of this work was publicly released (International Platform on Sustainable Finance, 2022), but it has not been validated by any country or utilised as a common set of definitions. It is unclear how this work will progress in the future, but for now it is fair to conclude that it has not had any impact in terms of mobilising private sector finance.

A third red flag is the potential for self-interest and corporate / economic interference to water down the definitions within each jurisdiction. As we have seen from the EU process, there is a risk that the taxonomy negotiation process becomes heavily influenced by industry and economic interests, rather than being based on scientific evidence as to what is a transition or adaptation activity. This lends itself to corporate interference, where the dominant industries in different regions place pressure on stakeholders (including governments) as part of the 'dialogue and engagement' process to water down the recommendations so that it doesn't harm or penalise their industry or economy. The controversial decision to include gas and nuclear as climate transition assets in the EU taxonomy is one example of this, palm oil plantations being included in the Malaysian Principles Based Taxonomy is another, as is South Africa following the EU approach by reportedly treating gas as a transition asset. Each jurisdiction will have its own agenda, so the watering down of the definitions not only move away from being 'common definitions' across jurisdictions, but the taxonomies also move away from representing what genuinely is a sustainability activity (according to scientific evidence, not economic interests).

So, we have several reasons why the taxonomy process could have very little impact on capital allocation flows into climate finance from the finance sector in the timeframe that is required. Can we apply our minds to think about this challenge through a broader lens? If we revisit one of the original goals behind the taxonomy process, which was to develop a common set of definitions to guide capital allocation decisions for financial institutions, might there be an alternative way to approach this challenge that would be: a) less time intensive and hence quicker to impact on capital allocation decisions; b) based on rigorous science, and hence consistent across sectors and regions; and c) reported and measurable, to improve transparency. Some of these questions are explored in Chapter 7 when we apply the mindset framework to look at this challenge through a different lens.

Lack of expertise

A number of industry and academic studies that have attempted to unravel the barriers to sustainable investment, including the mobilisation of capital into climate finance, have identified a lack of expertise as a possible obstacle. Here are some of the observations that have been made:

> *"Institutional investors often lack the resources and experience, particularly in private markets, to commit substantial capital."*
> Source: PRI (2022:12)

> *"Barriers to private investment in green infrastructure include lack of familiarity, limited information and knowledge, and limited expertise on green infrastructure."*
> Source: OECD (2021:1)

There is somewhat of a paradox in this explanation for inaction, as the financial sector is one of the most highly trained and compensated professions in the world, often praised (and/or pilloried) for being creative and innovative in generating financial returns from almost any situation. Indeed, there is a widely used term aka 'smart money' of which institutional investors and other professional investors are included, meaning that they have a fuller understanding of the market and a better chance of success in investing compared to non-expert investors. Despite this base of expert knowledge, when it comes to financing climate change activities, the indications are that there may be a knowledge gap or that more experience is needed.

It would be impossible to estimate the multitude of industry guides and reports have been produced by the various investor networks (such as the PRI, UNEP FI, IIGCC, Ceres, ICCC, CDP) to try to build this knowledge base through case studies and practical tools. The CFA Institute has also embedded sustainability into its training as have most universities around the world across a multitude of disciplines, including finance and economics. The central banks through the Network for Greening the Financial System are also making their contributions. However, the knowledge gap still arises as an explanation in different contexts to explain one of the barriers to capital allocation.

Lack of knowledge on climate change would now be viewed as a failure to adequately exercise fiduciary duty in a world where there is a voluminous quantity of information, evidence and data on climate mitigation and adaptation. Certainly, the risks of claiming not to know about the issue are higher than denying it exists. It is well documented and agreed that the financial flows to combat climate change and adapt to its effects are a vital part of the actions that are needed, and that the financial sector plays a central role in closing the financing gap. Any financial institution that has committed to align with or support a just and fair Net Zero by 2050 pathway and climate resilience and who is failing to allocate capital to combat the problem is clearly behaving in a contradictory manner, which will be a harder position to justify as the scrutiny on climate finance intensifies.

A final point of note, wilful blindness is another possible explanation underpinning the 'lack of expertise' explanation. As Heffernan (2019) observed, there is a tendency for people to ignore the obvious to feel safe, avoid conflict, reduce anxiety, and protect prestige. We will return to this topic in Chapter 7 to further explore ways to approach the possible fear of failure when it comes to capital allocation to climate finance.

Liquidity barriers

Another barrier to climate financing that often arises in analysis of the challenges from the perspective of financial institutions is the illiquid nature of many investment opportunities. To put this into context, financial institutions must comply with various capital requirements that exist for different types of financial institutions and jurisdictions that limit how much capital can be invested in illiquid assets. As the OECD (2021) noted, many of the investment opportunities are focused on mitigation and adaptation in infrastructure assets, which tend to be long-term in nature and illiquid, with nascent secondary markets that need to be deepened. The OECD also noted that this is true for developing economies and is even more pronounced in the emerging market and developing economies where the financing needs are also the greatest.

To recap some relevant observations made in Chapter 4, the Climate Policy Initiative data showed that the dominant financing instrument for climate finance activities by commercial institutions (retail and investment banks) are currently balance sheet debt financing and project-level debt, whereas for corporations the instruments are balance sheet equity financing and project-level equity. For institutional investors, the dominant financing instrument is project-level equity and debt (green bonds), with some balance sheet financing albeit a much small proportion. The BNEF data reaffirmed these observations, showing that asset finance still makes up the lion's share of new private sector investments in renewable energy, with public markets and PE/VC making only a very minor contribution.

What this means is that, as it stands today, institutional investors who rely on investing through 'fund' structures and who must comply with regulatory constraints regarding liquidity and capital requirements are constrained in how much capital can be allocated to such opportunities. To invest in climate finance currently, investors need to expand their investments into project finance, green bonds and other (predominantly) illiquid asset classes, such as sustainable agriculture, sustainable timberland, green infrastructure, green and climate efficient buildings and green private equity/private debt. There are new equity index funds that are focused on sustainability issues, although many of these have a broader remit than climate finance and tend to result in a broad-ranged set of exposures into companies with higher ESG 'scores', higher green revenue, or low carbon footprints. In this way, the universe is still directed towards minimising harm, rather than investing in the solutions that are needed to mitigate and adapt to climate change.

These are challenges that have been widely debated in the industry and amongst financial regulators for some time, with calls for consideration of actions such as preferential capital requirements for climate finance activities (European Banking Federation, 2017), collaboration between private and public sector agencies (including development banks) to build secondary market liquidity (OECD, 2021), and other forms of blended finance between different types of financiers (public, private and DFIs for example) to build alternative structures to access the investments through funds structures and third party managers (BloombergNEF, 2021).

Whilst liquidity needs are real and present, this issue could also be viewed as a transitory constraint as the market depth and breadth expands (as is the case for any new or growing market). However, clearly the climate financing gap must be addressed with urgency, and escalated action is needed to redress what is in effect, a form of market failure.

In addition to the easing of regulations, collaboration, and blended finance approaches that the industry is rightly pursuing, further questions that invite an exploration of how we think about this perceived barrier is explored in Chapter 7. For example, investors could consider how they can reorient their internal processes to prioritise the allocation of capital to climate finance opportunities versus other types of illiquid assets that they might consider. This could help to divert not only new fund inflows into climate finance activities, but it could also steer the redemptions of existing investments in illiquid assets into climate finance. In addition, investors could build expertise to invest more capital into primary and direct climate finance investments, compared to the more typical fund and third-party structures. As Chapter 7 suggests, can we develop new, innovative solutions - or new ways to think about old problems, differently?

Excessive deal pricing

Another factor that has been identified by some investors when considering capital allocation to climate finance opportunities is the excessive pricing of some climate mitigation assets. It is not straightforward to examine this claim, as we have seen, many of the deals are still project finance based and hence there is limited visibility on pricing. However, there is evidence of market pricing via the green bond market that we can examine and a raft of anecdotal evidence that we can reflect on.

Starting with the green bond market, the consensus opinion and research on this topic suggests that a green premium of between 1-9 bps exists for green bonds, meaning that the price is higher and the yield lower for comparable assets of the same duration and credit rating (MacAskill et al, 2021). The evidence in listed equities (IEA, 2021) also indicates that a premium for renewable energy assets versus fossil fuels can be found on average over the past decade, although unusual conditions have impacted on the energy markets in that time including COVID-19 and the Russian invasion of Ukraine. Nevertheless, the evidence suggests that there is a premium being paid for some green assets in both the bond and equity markets.

In terms of project financing and infrastructure, there is evidence that the cost of capital for renewable energy and energy efficient projects have fallen, while at the same time increasing considerable for coal related assets and other fossil fuel projects (Fattouh et al, 2019); with some examples of the cost of capital for coal related assets being 4x the cost of renewable energy projects.

The explanation for this pricing is straightforward; demand for green assets is outpacing supply due to the climate mitigation trajectory that the global economy is on, hence the price of such assets is being driven up. This is a cyclical and/or temporary phenomenon, as increased supply will catch up to demand and readjust market pricing (Blanc-Brude and Amenc, 2022). It is also not universal, as some assets will be priced excessively, and others may not. It is possible, however, that the mispricing may persist for some time yet, depending on the speed at which the projects and deal flow proliferates from here.

As Chapter 7 explores, if we adopt the mindset of a deal maker, not a deal taker, will the concerns about excessive pricing be as prevalent? The question invites a more pro-active approach to capital allocation, rather than lining up alongside other investors to invest in a structure that is ready made, can we be a primary market investor in these opportunities, what that would look like and involve in terms of internal capital allocation processes?

Difficult to access

Another prominent explanation for slowing down climate finance is the difficulty in accessing these investment opportunities. The combined effect of the concentration of investment needs in emerging and developing countries where local knowledge and networks are key, the 'off market' nature of the project-based deal flow, the lack of liquid and 'fund' based solutions and the sometimes-small scale of the investments, are often cited by investors in various forums on this topic (Carney, 2020; PRI, 2022; and Bloomberg NEF, 2022).

The work of some of the GZANZ members on this topic is targeting these specific challenges, with clear solutions and a pathway for reducing the access issues for investors. Some examples of this work include the establishment of FAST-Infra - Finance to Accelerate Sustainable Transition in Infrastructure (FAST-Infra) (Climate Policy Initiative, 2021). This is a collaboration between HSBC, the OECD, the IFC, the Global Infrastructure Facility (GIF) and the Climate Policy Initiative to make sustainable investment in infrastructure accessible. It is supported by more than 80 public and private institutions and focuses on each of the obstacles that have been identified, including the importance of local networks and knowledge, increasing visibility on deal flow, and improving the options for accessing these deals.

The GFANZ network also recommended to G20 leaders that a country platform-based approach be adopted to address the climate financing gap in each jurisdiction. A detailed set of recommendations for both policy makers and the financial sector in each country was proposed (GFANZ, 2023), with examples of such activities already underway in Columbia and India (Climate Finance Leadership Initiative, 2023). A study focused on the opportunities in climate mitigation investment in the EMDEs for Australian based investors also set out several detailed recommendations and pathways for action, including blended finance, increasing offtake certainty, and investing via debt or pooled funds to minimise risk (IGCC, 2023).

It seems there are some very well considered frameworks and recommendations that have been put forward by reputable organisations and people inside the financial sector, and indeed commitments that have been made to address the challenges with accessing the opportunities in climate finance. The question for investors going forward is therefore how to best use and leverage this body of knowledge and guidance, as access to opportunities is no longer a tenable rationale for failing to do so. This is further explored in Chapter 7 as we apply the mindset framework.

Summary

This chapter has explored some of the most cited barriers to climate finance from the perspective of the financial sector. We have seen a raft of explanations that are often put forward to explain the slow pace of capital allocation, ranging from inconsistent government policies, lack of information and standardised definitions, lack of expertise, liquidity implications, excessive pricing, and difficulty in accessing opportunities.

Something that all the barriers have in common is that they are perceived to be conditions that impact on the external environment in which investors operate in, rather than something that investors themselves might be doing or could approach differently (the 'internal' conditions that we will discuss in the next chapter). The problem with this is that it can be easier for investors to unknowingly hide behind these apparent barriers as justification for inaction, although that position is getting more difficult to sustain over time.

All these challenges might be best described as transitory barriers, and not dissimilar to any new market opportunity that might arise. For example, the reported lack of information, common definitions, expertise, pricing anomalies, illiquidity and deal access are all

characteristics of any market that is new or unfamiliar. These are not justifiable reasons for inaction, rather they are a description of conditions that sophisticated investors need to work within when making investment decisions under uncertainty.
There is never any certainty when it comes to investment decision making, imperfect information is a well-accepted condition that prevails over every decision. The question is really whether there is sufficient information, tools, skills, and frameworks in place to support well-informed and justifiable decisions, and how much longer the reasons for not allocating capital to climate finance will be defensible, especially when made by investors who publicly state their support for achieving net zero and building climate resilience.

We will now turn to look at some of the internal barriers to climate financing, to explore some of the inner dimensions that influence how investors perceive the external world and their response to it. These are often issues that are overlooked or perhaps considered secondary to capital allocation processes, but as Chapter 3 illustrated, how we feel and think is incredibly important for how we behave and therefore, how investors' invest.

References

Alessi, L., Ossola, E. and Panzica, R. (2019). The Greenium matters: evidence on the pricing of climate risk. An unpublished discussion paper.

Australian Sustainable Finance Institute. (2023). Taxonomy project. www.asfi.org

Blanc-Brude, F., and Amenc, F. (2022). The Pricing of Green Infrastructure. Published by EDHEC Infrastructure & Private Assets Research Institute. Available: https://edhec.infrastructure.institute/paper/the-pricing-of-green-infrastructure/.

Bloomberg NEF. (2022). Mobilizing Capital into Emerging Markets and Developing Economies. Commissioned by GFANZ. Published by BloombergNEF. Available at: https://assets.bbhub.io/professional/sites/24/Mobilizing-Capital-to-EMDEs.pdf.

Cano, G., and Trivedi, G. (2020). Is there a green-to-fossil fuel premium? An article published by MSCI Research.

Carney, M. (2020). Building a financial system for net zero, Priorities for private finance for COP26. UN Special Envoy for Climate Action and Finance and the Prime Minister's Finance Adviser for COP26.

Climate Finance Leadership Initiative. (2023). Financing sustainable infrastructure in emerging markets. https://www.bloomberg.com/cfli/mobilizing-investment/.

Climate Policy Initiative. (2021). Fast Infrastructure Platform. https://www.climatepolicyinitiative.org/fast-infra/

European Banking Federation. (2017). Towards a Green Finance Framework. https://www.ebf.eu/wp-content/uploads/2017/09/Geen-finance-complete.pdf.

European Commission. (2023). EU taxonomy for sustainable activities.

Fattouh, B., Poudineh, R. & West, R. (2019). The rise of renewables and energy transition: what adaptation strategy exists for oil companies and oil-exporting countries? Energy Transit 3, 45–58. https://doi.org/10.1007/s41825-019-00013.

GFANZ. (2023). The potential for country platforms to mobilise capital for net-zero transitions in emerging markets and developing economies. Draft Private Sector Statement.

Heffernan, M. (2019). Wilful blindness: Why we ignore the obvious. London: Simon & Schuster.

IEA. (2021). Clean Energy Investing: Global Comparison of Investment Returns. An IEA publication. https://www.iea.org/reports/clean-energy-investing-global-comparison-of-investment-returns.

IGCC. (2023). Mobilising climate investment in emerging markets: Opportunities for Australian pension and superannuation funds. An IGCC publication.

IGCC. (2022). Making the Transition Happen: Investment policy for a net zero economy. An IGCC publication.

International Platform on Sustainable Finance. (2022). Common ground taxonomy. https://finance.ec.europa.eu/system/files/2022-06/220603-international-platform-sustainable-finance-common-ground-taxonomy-instruction-report_en.pdf

International Sustainability Standards Board. (2023). IFRS S2 Sustainability Disclosure Standard: Climate-related Disclosures. www.ifrs.org.

MacAskill, S., Roca, E., Liu, B., Stewart, R. A., and Sahin, O. (2021). Is there a green premium in the green bond market? Systematic literature review revealing premium determinants. Journal of Cleaner Production 280 (Part 2) 124491. https://doi.org/10.1016/j.jclepro.2020.124491.

OECD. (2021). De-risking institutional investment in green infrastructure: 2021 progress update. OECD Environment

Policy Papers, No. 28, OECD Publishing, Paris, https://doi.org/10.1787/357c027e-en.

OECD. (2015). Mobilising private investment in clean-energy infrastructure. An OECD publication. https://www.oecd.org/daf/inv/investment-policy/Private-investment-in-clean-energy-infrastructure.pdf.

OECD. (2013). Financing Climate Change Action. An OECD publication. www.oecd.org/env/cc/financing.

Pietsch, A. and Salakhova, D. (2022). Pricing of Green Bonds: Drivers and Dynamics of the Greenium. SSRN Electronic Journal. https://doi.org/10.2139/ssrn.4227559.

Principles for Responsible Investment. (2022). Closing the funding gap: The case for ESG incorporation and sustainability outcomes in emerging markets. Published by the PRI. Available at: https://www.unpri.org/sustainable-development-goals/closing-the-funding-gap-the-case-for-esg-incorporation-and-sustainability-outcomes-in-emerging-markets/9430.article.

S&P Global. (2022). What the inclusion of gas and nuclear in the EU taxonomy could mean for investors and asset managers. An article published by S&P Global. www.spglobal.com.

TCFD. (2022). TCFD Status Report: Task Force on Climate-related Financial Disclosures. www.fsb.org.

The Investor Agenda. (2022). Global Investor Statement to Governments on Climate Crisis. https://theinvestoragenda.org/wp-content/uploads/2022/08/2022-Global-Investor-Statement-.pdf.

Wass, S. (2021). Green bond greenium is evident globally, especially strong for US dollar debt. An article published by S&P Global market Intelligence.

5. Internal barriers to climate financing

"From the perspective of running our pension fund on a day-to-day basis, it can seem like this issue [climate change] can wait."
Quote from a CIO at a European pension fund [ClimateWorks, 2019]

"Tools exist to invest in climate change solutions, motivation tends to be the primary obstacle."
Quote from a CIO at a UK pension fund [ClimateWorks, 2019]

The internal barriers are much less widely discussed in the context of the financial sector and climate finance, although the industry is aware of some of these issues, particularly short-termism, as evidenced by the various long-term investing groups that have existed over time. Yet at the industry level - and indeed at the regulatory level – as we have seen in Chapter 2, proponents of investor action on climate change tend to focus more on fulfilling their external needs.

Very little attention is, in comparison, placed on how knowledge is processed by investors and interpreted through their mental models. The psychological underpinnings of investment decisions, the prevalence of cognitive biases, culture and personal relationships (both at the individual level and inside and outside organisations) and how these might impact on the level of action on climate change needs further attention. Putting it another way, the assumption that if decision makers 'have information, will act' is still predicated on the assumption of rationality, even when there is clear evidence that rationality is a theoretical construct rather than a description of our reality (Sunstein, 2018).

Unless we more explicitly acknowledge the human dimension of investment decisions, the investment community will fail to adequately address the sustainability challenges of our time, regardless of our good intentions or support for the SDGs and Net Zero by 2050. It is only with focused effort and a close look at the internal (as well as the external) conditions that will we genuinely begin to realise our sustainability goals, and to align our behaviour and decisions with the attainment of these goals.

It is for this reason that this chapter focuses on investors as humans who have bounded rationality and make decisions based on a range of influences (Simon, 1982). Many of these influences on decision making are related to 'internal' conditions and how the mind processes and responds to information. The chapter is divided into two parts: first, the relevant literature is explored, and a theoretical framework is set out. Second, evidence is presented from a research project on Institutional Investors and the *Behavioural Barriers to Taking Action on Climate Change* that that I co-authored with Julian Poulter, funded by ClimateWorks Foundation (ClimateWorks, 2019).

Relevant literature

There is a growing body of academic and industry literature on the behavioural barriers that limit climate change action. Most of the research does not directly address the institutional investor community (with a few exceptions (Daumas, 2023), rather it focuses on the role of consumers and political agents in mitigating climate change. Nevertheless, there is a plethora of research and literature relevant to better understanding the behavioural barriers to acting on climate change that can be drawn upon, as presented in Figure 18.

Figure 18. Internal barriers to climate financing

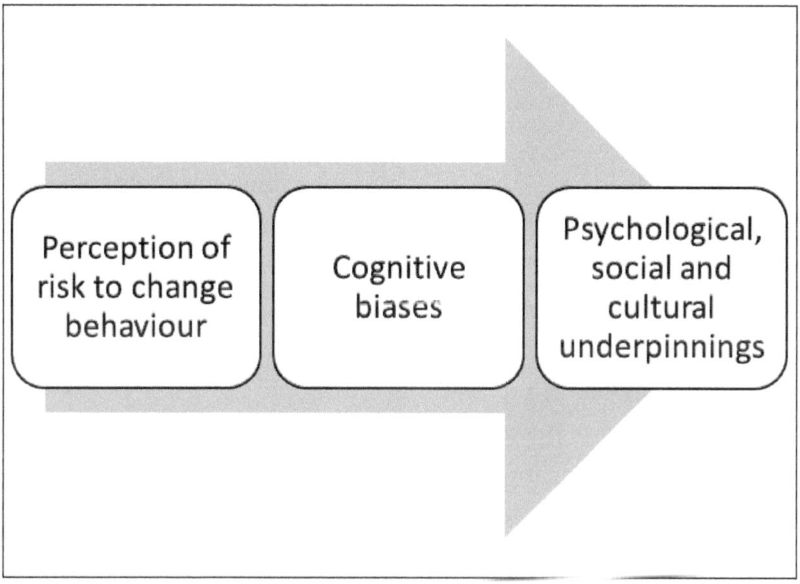

Source: Adapted from ClimateWorks (2019)

- **Perception of risk:** Understand investors' perception of risk associated with changing behaviour to incorporate climate-related impacts into valuation frameworks, portfolio construction and investment decision-making processes.
- **Cognitive biases:** Consider the prevalence of behavioural biases (short termism, heuristics, herding and cognitive dissonance) to understand some of the practical challenges to shifting behaviour.

- **Psychological, social and cultural underpinnings:** Understand the psychological, social and cultural influences that impact on the extent to which investors are willing and/or able to incorporate climate change into investment processes.

Efficient market hypothesis and market pricing

When it comes to addressing systemic risks such as climate change, the assumption that the market can price in complexity and uncertainty in a rational and orderly way needs to be revisited. Indeed, the work of many economic psychologists and behavioural financiers suggests that human behaviour does not always conform to the expected behaviour of a rational economic agent, and financial assets are not always able to reflect all public information correctly. Indeed, asset prices can be mispriced for a significant period, often resulting in bubbles in asset prices that precede a collapse; the technology bubble and the global financial crisis being recent examples of these tendencies.

Violations of the efficient and rational market model have been found to be systematic, robust, and fundamental, suggesting that we may need a new paradigm that reflects investor behaviour and how markets operate. Indeed, as Shiller (2005) observed, there can be periods where it is obvious to some that there is a systemic mispricing of asset values, yet such a situation can persist for some time. The awareness by some (perhaps the so-called 'smart money') that a mispricing exists does not necessarily mean that such a situation will be corrected any time soon. As Shiller (2005) noted in relation to over-priced assets in the lead up to the bursting of the technology bubble in 1999/2000:

> *"Those who doubt the value of these [mis-priced] stocks could try to sell them short…but their willingness to do so is limited,*

> *partly since there is always a possibility that the stock would be bid up even further by enthusiastic investors.... Absurd prices sometimes last a long time."*
> Shiller (2005:181)

All of this points to a greater level of complexity when we think about investors that are behind the investment decisions than the Efficient Markets Hypothesis (EMH) allows for. In the context of climate change, there is a growing sense of concern and evidence of the potential for some high carbon assets to become stranded or significantly re-priced downwards in view of the emerging policy and technology shifts to support the shift to a low carbon economy. Likewise, many low carbon assets may not have fully priced in their (true) long-term potential upside in a carbon constrained world.

The perception around market pricing or climate risk is informative as it indicates the extent to which investors believe (or not) there is a persistent market mispricing that does not adequately incorporate climate-related impacts. According to the EMH, a rational response to persistent market mispricing would be to exploit or position portfolios to take advantage of that situation. When a mispricing persists whilst the awareness of such a situation is building amongst investors, it suggests there are barriers to market re-pricing beyond purely technical or information-based explanations, including cognitive, psychological, cultural and social influences (Shiller, 2005).

Perception of risk

Beyond the volatility of financial returns, investors' perception of risk is also influenced by considerations such as career risk, peer risk, reputation risk – or as Keynes aptly observed in the beauty context analogy – the fear of being different to consensus and being wrong:

> *"Worldly wisdom teaches that is it is better for reputation to fail conventionally than to succeed unconventionally." (Keynes, 1936)*

In the context of climate change and investment decisions, taking a pro-active stance on the issue and/or adapting investment frameworks that differ from the prevailing market norms brings a perceived risk of failure, if such an approach results in lower investment returns.

Indeed, the perception of risk has been identified by psychologists and behaviouralists as a key driver that impacts on an individuals' willingness to act on climate change, both at the conscious and unconscious level. Van der Linden (2017) proposed a useful schematic that attempts to bring the strands of risk perception research together into a unified framework that can be used to measure and operationalise risk perception. This included a distinction between social and personal level judgements (will it impact more broadly, versus am I personally at risk). As Figure 19 summarises, changing behaviour brings perceived risks that are multi-dimensional (Carvalho, 2010; APA, 2009 and Van der Linden, 2017).

These are important insights for researching investor behaviour and climate change, as perception of risk is a key driver of investor behaviour across all investment issues, not only climate change. These insights were reflected in the design of the survey on investor behaviour (Annexure A) to gauge the perception of risk in relation to climate change (both the perception of risk from acting, and from not taking action).

Figure 19. Perceived risks of changing behaviour

- Functional (perceived control, my actions might not work, not sure how to do it, too many options).
- Financial (loss aversion, it might cost me money to act and endowment effect, I don't want to give up on what I already have).
- Psychological, social and cultural (this makes me feel uncomfortable, it is outside my comfort zone, not directly relevant to me others are not taking action, it might harm my reputation).
- Cognitive (heuristics or rules of thumb, it doesn't fit into my day-to-day activities, it is complex and difficult, requires a lot of effort).

Cognitive biases

Behavioural finance, economic psychology and related disciplines have identified several cognitive biases that may impact on how investors make decisions that further challenge the assumptions of the EMH and rationality. Many, though not all, have relevance for how investors respond to managing climate change risks and opportunities. Four biases that are of particular interest and relevance for examining the internal barriers to capital allocation to climate finance include:

i. **Myopia** (or short-termism), there is growing evidence and recognition across the investment and regulatory communities that the short-term time horizon of investors and the market more broadly is problematic when addressing systemic issues such as climate change than span multiple horizons. This will potentially impact on agents along the investment chain, including asset managers, asset owners, CIOs, Boards and Trustees to the extent that short-term performance is given precedence or priority over longer-term outcomes and risks.

ii. The **heuristics or rules of thumb** tendency to rely on a narrow set of parameters or guideposts to underpin decisions as researched through the seminal work of Tversky and Kahneman (1982) and latterly Thaler, Sunstein & Balz (2013) who coined the term "choice architecture" where people prefer simplicity, have a limited attention span, and go out of their way to avoid hassles. This tendency to simplify decisions could potentially thwart efforts to integrate climate change into investment processes. This relates also to narrow framing, where investors seek to reduce the complexity of their decisions, particularly the case for Boards and Trustees where there is limited time when the Board comes together and hence may have less capacity to go deeper into issues such as climate change.

iii. **Herding, group think**, or gravitation to defensible decisions, where investors have the tendency to mimic the behaviour of others and act according to the "rules of the game", whether consciously or unconsciously. As the Keynes beauty contest analogy posited, there is safety in numbers, if everyone gets it wrong then they all go down together, there is less reputational risk than going alone. To the extent that climate change is not yet 'conventional' amongst investors in terms of day-to-day investment decision making, it may feel riskier for investors to take decisive action (although it is increasingly become part of their rhetoric which is an indicator that change in market conventions and groupthink are underway). This applies to all layers of the investment decision chain, for fund managers and CIOs it is about potential impact on relative performance against benchmarks and potentially their reputation, for trustees and Boards it is fear of litigation risk, reputation and/ or a performance penalty.

iv. **Cognitive dissonance** or inconsistency, whereby conflicting attitudes, behaviours, and beliefs produce a feeling of discomfort, which can result in an alteration or internal shift in some way (Festinger, 1957). In the context of climate change and investor action this is highly relevant, particularly as awareness of the scale and magnitude of the challenge continues to spread. However, the emergence of a tension between attitudes and behaviour does not automatically mean that decisive action on climate change will emerge. Indeed, when a feeling of discomfort or dissonance arises, there are multiple ways for people to respond, such as pushing it away, denying it, becoming defensive or even going back and questioning or placing doubt on the initial cognitive judgement that caused the feeling of discomfort, rather than admitting they were wrong (Schneider, Gruman, & Coutts, 2005).

A better understanding of how investors think about capital allocation to climate change, the underlying psychological drivers to their response, attitudes, and behaviour (and the internal inconsistency or dissonance that exists between these responses) are all vital to better understand the gap between beliefs and action (that go beyond external conditions).

Psychological, social and cultural underpinnings

Not all behavioural anomalies can be fully understood by considering individual heuristics, rules of thumb and other non-random biases, we must also consider the social, cultural, organisation, political economy and market-wide contexts in which decisions are being made to fully understand investor behaviour. Insights from economic psychologists such as Farr (1997) and Lewis (2001) remind us that beliefs and values (that ultimately influence decision making, are shared with others and are a social, not an individual, phenomenon. Indeed, this was an important observation made by Keynes, namely that decisions to invest are largely governed by the average expectation of the market, rather than the genuine expectation of the investor. Therefore, to reduce and manage uncertainty, investors rely on the maintenance of an industry convention that can be relied upon, even if it sustains unhelpful behaviours and outcomes.

> *"Thus, investment becomes reasonably 'safe' for the individual investor over short periods, and hence over a succession of short periods however many, if he can fairly rely on there being no breakdown in the convention and on his therefore having an opportunity to revise his judgement and change his investment,*

> *before there has been time for much to happen. Investment which are 'fixed' for the community are thus made 'liquid' for the individual."*
> (Keynes, 1936:153)

With climate change not yet a 'conventional' and widely accepted core driver of company or asset valuations, creating a need for affirmation from the wider market around its legitimacy, potentially acting as a barrier to increased capital allocation to climate mitigation and adaptation activities (until we reach the point of critical mass).

> The interdependency between investors, the role of expectations formation and the influence of others on decision making as observed by Keynes are all conditions that will support behaviour and expectations formation that renders climate change a 'conventional' part of the capital allocation process.

Norgaard (2006) identified several psychological barriers in responding to climate change and classified these in terms of identified barriers versus the underlying drivers. Norgaard focuses on "knowing and not knowing" where society has the information, but most people are not thinking about climate change in their everyday lives. Another wide-ranging review of the psychological, social, and cultural underpinnings that limit climate change action was carried out by the APA (2009), which identified a sequence of barriers as summarised in Highlight.

Highlight: Psychological, social and cultural barriers that limit climate change action

- Ignorance and uncertainty – informational barriers, lack of awareness and underestimation of the risks.
- Mistrust and reactance – people do not trust the message, skeptical.
- Denial – belief that they cannot do anything about it, perhaps a deeper fear of mortality.
- Judgmental discounting – belief that changes can be made in the future; it is worse elsewhere.
- Habit – this is how we do things around here; I've always done it this way.
- Perceived control – belief that they have little control over the outcome, defeatist.
- Perceived risks – changing behaviour brings risks (see perception of risk discussion).
- Tokenism – take some token action, no real meaningful change.
- Social comparison and norms – compare their actions to others (Festinger, 1954), peer norms a strong influence.
- Conflicting goals – having multiple goals and values that are perceived to be conflicting.
- Belief in solutions – belief that others will take care of it; it will be ok.

Source: http://www.apa.org/science/about/publications/climate-change.aspx

Evidence

This section summarises the findings of a research project on Institutional Investors and the Behavioural Barriers to *Taking Action on Climate Change* that that was co-authored with Julian Poulter, funded by ClimateWorks Foundation (ClimateWorks, 2019). The study analysed the behavioural drivers that impact on institutional investors' ability and/or willingness to integrate climate-related risks and opportunities into their investment decisions.

As this section will demonstrate, evidence of cognitive biases and psychological underpinnings was discovered, including myopia, herding and reliance on heuristics and rules of thumb. In addition, open-ended responses to a survey and follow up interviews revealed the importance of other behavioural biases including cognitive dissonance, narrow framing, loss aversion, status quo bias and overconfidence.

In short, the data collection and analysis of the research was conducted in 6 main stages:

1. Review of relevant research and evidence
2. Design and distribute a survey to institutional investors (globally, across function)
3. Undertake interviews with CIOs/CEOs and senior staff inside financial institutions
4. Examine the findings and distill key themes
5. Consider the implications for stakeholders
6. Suggest recommendations and next steps

Survey design and findings

As part of the study, a survey was developed to gauge and better understand the prevalence of some of the behavioural barriers amongst institutional investors when it comes to acting on climate change (Annexure A). The survey was distributed to institutional investors internationally through social media and industry networks and received 89 responses in total, spread across 6 regions and all layers of the investment management chain in terms of function (analysts, strategists, portfolio managers, CIOs, CEOs, Board members, trustees, department heads, ESG specialists, advisors, researchers, data providers), including asset owners (29%), asset managers (24%), investment consultants (9%), investment banks (2%), service providers (15%), independent advisors (10%) and other (11%). Two thirds of respondents were male, one third female, with the median age in the 35-54 range.

Aggregate survey findings

Some of the key findings from the survey are summarised in Figure 20, mapped alongside each of the cognitive and psychological underpinnings. After the first profile-based questions, the survey started off by gauging general beliefs about climate change, before moving on to examine more specific considerations to reveal any discrepancies and/or deeper insights into these beliefs in terms of how they might impact on behaviour and perception of risk.

Figure 20. Aggregate survey findings

Theme	Key findings	Cognitive biases	Psychological underpinnings
Disconnect from beliefs and broader purpose	There is general acknowledgment of climate change as a systemic risk, but in practice at the day-to-day level, there is a degree of separation from the issue in terms of their sense of purpose	Myopia, cognitive dissonance	Uncertainty, denial, judgmental discounting, perceived control
Uncomfortable with complexity	There is growing effort and momentum in some areas (such as engagement with companies on climate change), yet it is complex and hard to incorporate into investment analysis	Narrow framing, heuristics, loss aversion	Habit, conflicting goals
Conforming to peer group	People do not think their peers are taking strong action on this issue in terms of capital allocation, there is a lack of motivation to go beyond what others are doing	Herding, loss aversion	Social comparison, norms, conformity
Failure to reflect on personal agency	When it comes to taking action to try to change "the other" (external fund managers or companies) then it is perceived to be easier. When it comes to changing their own practices (i.e., valuation frameworks or capital allocation decisions) then that is considered to be much more difficult	Status quo bias, narrow framing	Denial, lack of self-awareness

Not embedded into culture	Climate change is generally not high on the priority in day-to-day decision-making processes, perception that specialist teams take care of those issues	Status quo bias, confirmation basis, recency bias	Adherence to team norms, conventions, habit, denial
Tension between the short and long term	There was a recognition that climate change exists and is in the background, although the shorter-term focus on financial performance can override these concerns which are perceived to be longer term	Overconfidence effect, myopia	Habit, social comparison, norms and conformity, conflicting goals,
Fear of failure	Some people felt that it can be very difficult to evaluate climate change impacts and takes more time and energy and motivation to change investment frameworks, and will also be harder to justify if it goes wrong	Heuristics, rules of thumb, anchoring	Fear of failure, habit, perceived risk of taking action, mistrust

Source: ClimateWorks (2019)

Beliefs

Survey question 6 was designed to gauge the overall beliefs with respect to climate change and its relative priority in the context of portfolio management decisions.

- There was general agreement that climate change poses a "serious risk that needs to be addressed urgently", with 64% strongly agreeing and 27% agreeing with this statement. Only 1% strongly disagreed.
- Moreover, 72% of respondents strongly agree that "taking action now will reduce future costs", with only 2% strongly disagreeing with this statement.

- There was general agreement also that investors can do something about this, with 90% of respondents either strongly agreeing or agreeing that climate change "provides new opportunities for investors."
- Nearly 90% of respondents disagreed or strongly disagreed with the statement that climate change "is too far into the future to assess" or that "there is little that investors can realistically do" about the issue."
- The response to the statement that "there are more pressing issues to address" than climate change generated a more mixed view, with around a third neither agreeing or disagreeing with this statement.

On the face of it, these results are very favourable and indicative of support for climate change action. This could be due to a selection bias to the respondents (where the respondents that completed the survey on balance also held a more supportive view of climate change). It could also be the first insight into revealing a possible gap between beliefs and behaviours and the emergence of cognitive dissonance which we further examine.

When we examined the open-ended responses to question 6, we observed layers of complexity to explain the responses that suggested the beliefs might not be as straightforward as initially suggested. For example, there was mention of a "*tension*" that existed in acting on long-term, chronic issues such as climate change. While it was seen as a "top 5" issue, by another, there are multiple and "equally pressing" issues that also need to be addressed. One even went as far to say that:

"…From the perspective of running our pension fund on a day-to-day basis, it can seem like this issue can wait."

We can see the prevalence of "knowing and not knowing" (Norgaard, 2010) and inconsistency reveal itself. Yes, there is general acknowledgment of climate change as a systemic risk, but in practice at the day-to-day level, there is a degree of separation from the issue in terms of what that means in practice. This observed prevalence of cognitive dissonance produces many potential consequences in terms of understanding the barriers and shifting investor behaviour that are further examined.

Complexity

Survey question 7 focused on the perceived level of difficulty associated with incorporating climate change into investment frameworks, to gain insight into the role that mental models, heuristics and rules of thumb play in taking action on climate change.

- The majority of respondents (45%) reportedly felt that "incorporating climate change into investment frameworks" was either difficult or very difficult. Around a third felt that it was neither easy nor difficult, with only 3% thinking it was very easy.
- So, while in the previous question it seemed that the majority of respondents felt that climate change could be acted upon, that it presented both opportunities and risks that could be managed today, when taken further, it seems that people think this is quite difficult to do (albeit not impossible).

Interestingly, the responses to the open-ended component of this question revealed an array of perspectives, we are seeing much more diversity in thinking already from the preceding question. For example, where external drivers were seen to be the most important difficulty with acting by some (citing lack of regulations, information, data, tools) others pointed to internal drivers, observing that it is "hard" to change existing frameworks in large organisations and that the:

> *"…tools exist, motivation tends to be the primary obstacle."*

Another respondent observed that:

> *"…existing frameworks have often developed over time, and so may require retooling, which can be labour intensive. Equally, adopting a single approach across sectors can be hard, particularly in large organisations."*

> These insights suggest that there is a degree of resistance to change existing frameworks, it takes time and energy and motivation to see it through, which may not be present. No amount of new tools or data will (in itself) address this obstacle, this is a barrier related to internal change at the individual (whether motivation exists) and organisation level (the effort needed to review existing frameworks). An expansion of heuristics and rules of thumb that embeds climate change will take conscious effort, time and motivation, clearly some of the respondents felt that the tools were increasingly available to support this shift. Others pointed to the internal challenges such as the weak level of commitment and the high level of effort required to utilise these tools and change processes.

Peer group

Survey question 8 considered the extent to which investors felt that their peers were acting on climate change, to gain insight into the behavioural tendency towards herding and to compare oneself to others, to feel more comfortable taking action that is perceived to be conventional.

- The majority of respondents (65%) felt that "climate change was being addressed by other investors, including peers 'to a very little' or 'somewhat' extent. Only 1% thought that it was being addressed to a 'great' extent.
- This lack of peer pressure or sense that other investors are not really taking strong action on climate change will also undermine the willingness and motivation to act.

Indeed, some of the open-ended responses pointed out that while there is growing effort and momentum across the industry and amongst their peers around some approaches (such as engagement with companies), many felt that climate change is:

> *"...not really incorporated into investment analysis."*

While some noted that there is more attention and talk about climate change, there is still:

> *"...not a lot of internal capabilities that would amount to serious action."*

There appears to be a general perception that the industry momentum on climate change and level of activity amongst peers has not resulted in meaningful change in terms of integration into investment analysis or building internal capabilities to take 'serious action'. This could undermine the motivation for some investors to review their own internal planning, prioritisation and climate-related actions.

Personal agency

Building on Question 7, Question 9 made efforts to go further to gauge attitudes towards specific actions that can be taken with respect to climate change.

- The most revealing insight from this question was that some activities were considered by most (more than 70% of respondents) to be either very easy or easy, namely engaging with external managers, engaging with companies and investing in low carbon opportunities.
- On the other end of the spectrum, integrating climate change into valuations, undertaking scenario analysis and reviewing asset allocation assumptions were identified as the most difficult or very difficult action to take by more than 60% of respondents.

This suggests that when it comes to taking action to try to change "the other" (external fund managers or companies) then it is easier. When it comes to changing themselves (i.e. their valuation frameworks or asset allocation models) then that is considered to be much more difficult. For example, one respondent noted that:

> *"...it is easy to incorporate but harder to actually implement climate change strategies into investment frameworks."*

Another observed the difference layers of integration:

> *"I think [climate change] is addressed by engagement but not really incorporated in investment analysis."*

With another suggesting that collective action is preferable:

> *"...it is a complex challenge and requires a broad range of responses....it is a collective action problem so success is not within the control of any individual fund."*

> The survey results suggest that collective action is preferable to action at the individual fund level, perhaps explaining the support for engagement strategies together with other investors to take action without actually questioning their personal agency or changing the mental models and frameworks that are heavily relied upon inside organisations. It also points to the potential prevalence of the status quo bias in terms of investors resisting change to their own frameworks versus greater support and willingness to take action to change "the other".

Culture

Survey question 10 provided respondents with the opportunity to self-identify with a list of potential challenges that include both external and internal dimensions. It was designed to gain further insight into the way investors think about climate change and what might be impacting on their ability and/or willingness to integrate it into investment decisions.

- The factors that were identified by respondents as being

the most important challenges that they faced were threefold, namely: 1) "lack of comparable data" (with 60% of respondents pointing to this as being an important or very important challenge); 2) "the lack of internal buy-in" within their organization (more than 55% identifying this as being an important or very important factor) and the "high degree of complexity" that managing climate change involves (more than 50% ranked as important or very important).

- The lack of organizational buy-in indicates that there are aspects related to culture that are not supporting or enabling people inside the organization to act on climate change in their day-to-day decisions. The signals they are getting from within the organizational context in terms of team interactions and processes indicate that the issue should not be given priority compared to other issues.

> Interestingly, of the 3 dominant challenges that were identified by respondents, 2 of them relate to internal processes (lack of organisational buy-in and perceived complexity) and the third relates to external forces (lack of data). This highlights the important role that behavioural analysis and internal enquiry can play in assessing and overcoming the impediments to acting on climate change; alongside improving access to data and tools, reducing the perceived complexity and implementing processes to change the culture of organisations will help to prioritise climate change as an integral part of investment analysis.

The open-ended responses also revealed some commonalities that pointed to the lack of organisational culture that supported or enabled a higher priority to be given to climate change impacts. For example, one respondent noted in the context of their investment team meetings:

> *"...we don't really discuss climate change in team meetings, it is one of those issues we all know is out there and it crops up sometimes, but there are lots of other issues we tend to focus on."*

With another stated that:

> *"...the greatest challenge is a behavioural one, challenging the status quo and vested interests."*

With such insights and awareness of the inner drivers and behavioural obstacles apparently prevalent from within the investment community, it is somewhat perplexing that these issues have not been more explicitly researched and focused on as part of scaling up investor action on climate change. It might not be as straightforward (or perhaps as commercially appealing) as building new tools and databases, but it is clearly essential.

Investment horizon

Survey question 11 explored several possible responses to gauge investors' perceived "risks associated with integrating climate-related impacts into investment decisions."

- The highest rated risks associated with integrating climate change into investment decisions included: 1) too complex to evaluate (30% of respondents); 2) time and resource intensive (32% of respondents); 3) not well entrenched across the industry (28% of respondents); and 4) hard to defend if it goes wrong (27% of respondents).
- That means that more than half of the respondents identified

the lack of industry norms and how defensible decisions are (if they go wrong) on the basis of climate change impacts being the rationale.

- On the other end of the spectrum, the potential risk of breaching fiduciary duty was rated as not a risk or a low risk by more than 70% of respondents, suggesting that (within the sample of this survey at least) this is not acting as a perceived barrier to action. Getting fired and/or a lower bonus was also quite low down on the level of concern, with 67% of respondents putting this as a very low or low risk in terms of acting on climate change.

The potential impact of short time horizons and the impact that can have on behaviour was also identified as a barrier, with one respondent noting that:

> *"The issue I believe is that Funds are measured over a relative short period. The impact of legislative change is often not immediate. Therefore, Funds can invest and exist before value is affected."*

Another highlighted the potential impact on performance and time horizon, noting that:

> *"By the time performance risk is material and visible to investors it might be too late for us as a global society to stabilise the climate."*

> The responses suggest that greater focus is needed on reducing the perceived complexity of acting on climate change. While there is a realisation of the need (by some respondents) for investors to take pre-emptive action, not to wait until the signs

of climate change are visible and self-evident – there is a still a perception that such behaviour is not yet normalised and would be harder to defend if it went wrong.

Fear of failure

In contrast to the previous question, survey question 12 set out several possible responses to gauge investors' perceived "risks associated with NOT integrating climate-related impacts into investment decisions."

- Interestingly, there was more dispersion in the responses to this question than in the previous one, indicating that when it comes to not acting, there is less consensus on what that means (compared to the risks of actually taking action).
- There were five risks that stood out as posing more concern amongst the majority of respondents than others in terms of not taking action on climate change, these being: 1) reputation risk of not acting (50% of respondents); 2) losing leadership status (52% of respondents); 3) missing out on new opportunities (50% of respondents); 4) higher system wide risks (54% of respondents); and 5) weak signals for companies and governments to act (60% of respondents).

These findings suggest that the perceived risk of not acting is more likely to impact on reputation and status in the industry, rather than negatively impacting on performance (whereas taking action in the previous question, led to some fear of the negative performance implications).

Indeed, half the respondents did not think that failure to act on climate change would result in a less diversified portfolio (50% ranking this as not a risk or a very low risk). Clearly there is an element of inconsistency on this point that needs to be further explored, as most respondents reportedly saw climate change as a major systemic risk that needed to be managed (question 6), yet at the same time half of the respondents think that this will not impact on portfolio diversification. This appears to suggest cognitive dissonance is present, leading to denial of the potential portfolio risks of not acting.

This could be underpinned by confirmation bias, where existing models and frameworks that are used to evaluate portfolio diversification are not reviewed considering climate change, rather the more convenient conclusion (that confirms the reliance on current frameworks) is that portfolio resilience will not be impacted.

Open ended responses

At the end of the survey, a space was provided for open ended comments or insights on this topic more generally, generating a high number of entries by respondents (26 of the 89 respondents offered additional comments); which was not only very generous in terms of the respondents' time and effort, but it also provided a useful into our analysis and guidance as we prepared for the interview stage of the research.

- One respondent noted that *"a huge part of the problem is changing mindsets"*, another stated that *"culture is critical"* and that the *"culture of the investment community"* needs to evolve, with one respondent claiming we are in the midst of a *"moral crisis"*.

- This confirms our efforts to focus on behaviours and their drivers, including dominant mindsets, values and culture.

- Other respondents point to resourcing issues internally, where *"time and resource shortages are often quite acute."*
  — This reaffirms the survey findings that internal buy-in at the organization wide level is needed to help prioritise the issue and also overcome the internal barriers that may slow down action.

- Another respondent noted that the main problem was that *"Funds are measured over a relatively short period…Funds can invest and exit before value is affected."* Another noted that by the time climate risk is *"visible to investors"* it might be *"too late for us as a global society to stabilize the climate."*
  — The notion of tragedy of the horizons emerged mostly strongly in the open-ended responses and throughout the interview process. Interestingly, short termism is not something that the respondents felt that they were personally contributing to, it appeared to be a problem with "the market" or "others", rather than themselves.

- Other respondents highlighted the importance of policy and regulations to spur action with one stating that *"it should be mainly regulation led in the end"* and another noting that *"nothing has driven change quite like the regulator incorporating climate change into new requirements in the UK."* Another noted that *"without a price on carbon the risks are hard to assess, and progress is likely to remain too slow."*

- This framing of the issue is more typical of how the investment community talks about climate change barriers to action, it relies on change to the "external" conditions rather than to "internal" processes or ways of thinking.
- Ideally, regulatory change that also seeks to reflect the drivers of behaviour, culture and mindsets would help to bring the 'internal' cognitive processes into alignment with the 'external' conditions to support greater climate action.

Cognitive dissonance

The disaggregated analysis of the survey responses pointed to evidence of a growing dislocation within the investment community, suggesting that there is a fragmentation of culture emerging which could potentially destabilise the status quo and allow new perspectives to filter through the system.

To analyse this fragmentation, the survey responses were categorised in terms of i) Divergence within the investment community; ii) Denial of an internal inconsistency; iii) Defensiveness to justify the internal inconsistency; iv) Decisiveness amongst some, to taking strong action on climate change (Figure 21).

Figure 21. Cognitive dissonance processes of investors with respect to climate change

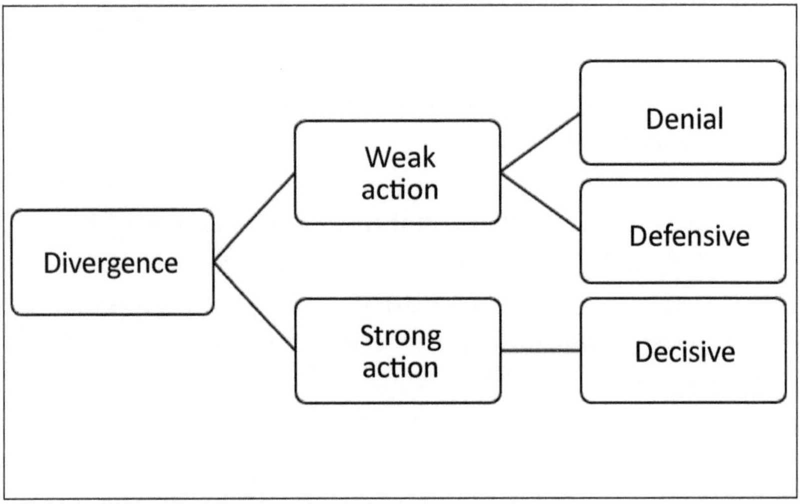

Source: ClimateWorks (2019:35)

- **Divergence** – Views within the investment community on what investor actions should be taken now in response to climate change are increasingly divergent.

While evidence was found of a generally accepted awareness and level of concern about climate change at the system wide level amongst investors, we also discovered a divergence in opinions about what that means in practice at the individual level. There is a sub-set of investors that have more strongly held beliefs and conviction than others, who are increasingly frustrated at the level of inaction.

Some of the open-ended responses highlight this emerging tension. For example, some comments that were made about senior investors inside organisations were:

> *"…too many excuses, a lot of talk but very little action. It should be mainly regulation led in the end."*

> *"…for the most part [they] are simply paying lip service to it…"*

> *"…the clever young turks should oust the lazy old lions..."*

- **Defensiveness** – Some investors appear to be less willing to take strong action now, they rely more heavily on perceived complexity to justify their position to themselves and to others.

Comments such as *"dealing with the here and now"* and *"managing as best we can with the information we have"* were the type of justifications that these investors gave for their more muted response.

One respondent noted that (underline added for emphasis):

> *"…<u>can</u> realistically do is not the same as <u>will</u> realistically do…"*

This suggests a level of awareness of the apparent gap between attitudes and behaviours, described as potential action and actual action. While action might be possible, there are all sorts of reasons why is might not be 'realistic' to go further.

- **Denial** – Although some acknowledge that climate change exists and revealed their concern at the system wide level - they demonstrated a degree of denial and disconnection from the issue in terms of its direct relevance to their day job.

As one respondent noted:

"This is a top five issue, but the plan faces multiple equally pressing issues."

The belief that climate change is an issue that sits alongside others, rather than representing a systemic risk of major proportions, reflects an element of denial of the evidence and a denial of their own attitude where almost all respondents highlighted it as a risk that needed to be managed with urgency (at the system wide level).

This tendency to disconnect from climate change at the individual (firm or organisation) level confirms existing research that points to a higher disconnection amongst those who feel they are a few steps removed from the brunt of the actual outcomes of climate change on them personally (Norgaard, 2010). In the case of our study, this disconnect manifests in terms of perceived threat (or not) to portfolio resilience and financial performance.

- **Decisiveness** – Some investors tended to have very strong views in favour of immediate and strong climate action, including through capital allocation.

Some investors were found to have stronger views on climate change, were less prone to cognitive biases and psychological barriers that thwarted their efforts and were more willing to act now. They demonstrated a strong motivation to act, referred less to tools, data, and information limitations and more about conviction, consistency, trust and building strong relationships to support and underpin their efforts.

This group has overcome the cognitive dissonance and come out the other side internally with a clear drive to act. The challenge for this group appears to be more related to managing a sense of frustration that they are insiders to the investment industry, they have a role to play, but their efforts are being undermined by the actions (or rather inaction) of others.

Some respondents noted that:

> *"Incorporation [of climate change] should be viewed as essential and require commitment to the necessary capacity building."*

> *"Institutions have other priorities where unhappily the means justify any way to reach them."*

> *"Too many influential asset owners and asset managers sit on the fence with enormous capital destruction looming."*

> *"I see climate change as posing global catastrophic dangers… while institutional investors have at their disposal substantial power to lead vital change through concerted political and financial engagement, this power must be more fully effectuated."*

Evidently these respondents spoke about climate change in a decisive way, there was little uncertainty as to how big the issue or challenge is, and also a clear demonstration of emotion and frustration at the lack of action. The "them and us" and why "they" should be doing more is also self-evident in terms of how they describe the issue.

This framework and evidence of cognitive dissonance could potentially support a theory of change, where the greater the divergence within the investment community, the harder it will be for resistant investors to continue responding to the prevalence of dissonance through denial or defensiveness. Not only will their own tribe feel like it is turning against them, the external pressure from their peers, beneficiaries, society (including voices in the youth movement), regulators, NGOs and other stakeholder groups will also add to the growing feeling of discomfort with existing positions and responses.

Interview design

The second research method utilised was a series of semi-structured 1:1 interviews with individuals inside institutional investment organisations.

A series of questions were developed to guide the interview process, although the approach taken was very much a semi-structured conversation as it was important to create an atmosphere of openness and trust, to better understand the issues from the perspective of the interviewees themselves on the links between real investor drivers and the underlying barriers to climate action. Indeed, the questions were not followed rigidly as the interviewees all had different perspectives on climate change and its implications for investment decisions, so this required judgement as to how best to ask and prioritise the questions in order to better understand their perspective.

To encourage the individuals to participate in the interview process, a project summary was prepared and sent as part of the invitation. Existing relationships with the individuals inside these organisations was important and there was certainly some selection bias in the interview list as we discovered that individuals inside organisations that were less 'progressed' in their thinking and actions on climate change were more reluctant to participate in the research.

> The reality is that existing leaders are far more prepared to talk about the barriers (and how they overcame them or are managing them presently) than less progressed investors who could feel more threatened or uncomfortable with discussing the challenges of taking action on climate change. More broadly, this is a challenge with any behavioural research undertaken on 'real world' people versus experimental or more theoretical approaches in the academic context.

With this sample bias in mind, the strategy that was adopted throughout the interview process was one of understanding the perspective of the interviewees, the challenges that they have (or are currently) encountering, how they manage and respond to these and how they see things evolving going forward. These insights from senior executives insider asset owner organisations are valuable to not only understand what strategies they employed to overcome some of the challenges that they encountered, but also to share these insights with other organisations that are less progressed on the journey. In this way, the herding tendency that was observed at the survey level could be a force for change, where the leading funds can help to pave the way for other investors to follow suit and evolve their own internal processes with respect to climate change. The power of the pack in challenging groupthink and industry norms is key.

A total of 8 teleconference interviews were carried out with individuals from different asset owner organisations, 7 of which represented executives at the CEO/CIO/Trustee level and

1 represented a senior responsible investment executive. All interviews were promised anonymity to encourage an open and frank dialogue.

Interview themes

During the interviews there were several themes that emerged in terms of how individuals in senior positions inside asset owner organisations have personally experienced the challenges with incorporating climate change into investment processes (n.b. italics indicates direct quotation from interviewees).

- **Information versus behavioural barriers:** No interviewees felt that the challenges with acting on climate change was purely due to lack of data or availability of models - or even policy or technology breakthroughs – all the interviewees talked about the importance of people, trust, and personal relationships inside their organisations.
  - Indeed, according to many of the interviewees, the volume of real-world evidence in policy, technology, weather, and science is helping to break down the barriers for not taking action.
  - One interviewee noted *"When towns start shutting down because of extreme weather, then surely that will change things. We are all going to die if we don't do anything, it's a scary trend"*.
  - Another interviewee noted the importance of the human dimension to investment, stating that *"Performance is achieved by individuals not by models"*.

- **Beliefs:** Personal belief provided a lot of the determination to do something different from their peers – not a moral or ethical belief but one steeped in the belief that climate is not going away, and that mitigation is the logical thing to do.

- Indeed, many of the interviewees indicated that most barriers have been overcome by a firm belief that this is happening and that the transition is inevitable.
- Leaders have a conviction that they will be rewarded at some point though they don't know when.
- All interviewees thought incentives were important but stressed It's more about the beliefs than incentives.
- One interviewee highlighted that conviction is key, noting that *"Our conviction that we are right on climate is stronger than our fear of failure"*.

- **Trust:** Strong overall fund / individual performance is a key element that allowed an individual to drive a pro-active climate agenda and develop a strategy. This performance creates trust from the board that allows the board to overcome any fears about risk in being unique or pro-active over climate.
  - Trust is key not only for approval of a climate change strategy but also to provide the delegated authority to implement it.
  - One interviewee noted that *"The decision making on how we implement the sustainable investing framework is ours – the board agree the framework and trust me to make the investments and they hold me accountable for those investment"*.
  - *"You need the CEO and CIO to have the mandate and trust from the board"*.

- **Culture:** Pressure on C-suite executives from even one or two board members is helpful to open up a dialogue on the issue, building a culture that embraces change and ultimately drives action.
  - To ensure positive climate behaviour, leaders emphasised the importance of having a culture that promotes and encourages people to do things differently.
  - Some leaders experienced early resistance from colleagues and board members, they thought it was making their life harder e.g., by implementing new benchmarks. However, it was explained that once the resisters (internally at the Board and executive level) had a chance to be heard they were less resistant. As one interviewee noted "*Once they had a chance to report their stance, they had an outlet, felt less sidelined and more listened to*".
  - Some simple processes can help overcome behavioural barriers such as focusing board conversations on 10 year returns rather than annual returns and performance on league tables.

- **Perception of risk:** The interviewees all felt that the degree of financial risk to become a leader was small. This is understood by the leaders who can allocate capital to low carbon assets and still take minimal career or reputational risk.
  - One interviewee noted that rather than being afraid of moving ahead of consensus opinion, this can actually work in favour of investment outcomes. "*There is a first mover advantage, risk adjusted returns are better if you go first*".

- Another interviewee explained the dynamic process and how perception of risk can change over time in regard to climate change. "*We saw our property portfolio lagging and thought maybe it was the green policies affecting performance, when we looked at it we could see it wasn't that but other sector drivers and forces. It then rebounded well, and we used it as an example to demonstrate to the board we needed to hold our nerve on sustainability*".

- **Finding the comfort zone:** There was some evidence of anchoring amongst the interviewees to what they feel most comfortable with. Most explained that it is far easier to expand a fund's climate strategy and invest in low carbon opportunities if the returns from existing investments are reasonable. According to most of the interviewees, the returns don't have to be higher than other areas, just comparable to other opportunities in similar asset classes.
  - One interviewee noted that "*other types of investments, not necessarily climate related, which have bounced back after poor periods provide a good precedent for maintaining faith in an existing climate strategy.*"
  - Almost all the interviewees didn't believe in divestment or negative screening.
  - As another interviewee noted, it is important to build a track record and knowledge over time for credibility and to reduce the difficulty of building a new program of investments, as "*CEO and CIOs can only allocate internal credibility effort to a certain number of issues*".
  - Overall fund performance is critical to acting, as one interviewee noted on performance "*Being a good performing fund is important to being able to act on climate.*

4th quartile investors don't want to take risks – they will head to a 3-year middle of the pack herd position to get themselves back up the ranking".

- **Reluctance to forecast:** Even the more progressive asset owners amongst those interviewed in this research have not gone as far as developing a public "base case" expectation for climate change yet, as they have been able to act without having to do this.
  - Our discussions indicated that to develop a fully-fledged "Paris aligned" base case would be to take a very big bet that most interviewees were reluctant to take. However, one CEO was so convinced about the future costs that will arise in the transition to a low carbon economy that he implemented fossil fuel free benchmarks across the entire equity portfolio. *"I put our forecast base case before the board, and they asked if I could guarantee that all my facts and figures were right and of course I could not, and you never can but they only ask this when you are trying to do something that your peers are not".*
  - The uncertainty around timing and reluctance to take a strong view or forecast the trajectory of climate change (and when the tipping point will be reached) is revealed as one interviewee explained that *"I think it has to flip in the next 5 years, but I've been wrong before. If you asked me 30, 20, 10 years etc you would have thought it would be sorted but we don't seem to be getting closer. It is impossible to tell when the tipping point might be. If I'd taken that view over the last 30 years I would have been consistently wrong".*

- **Peers:** Rather than feeling pressure to stay in the pack and not go too far from the 'norm', the leaders were often disparaging of peers who had failed to see the obvious risks or who were unwilling to overcome any fears or biases in order to act on climate change.
  - All interviewees recognised in their peers that it is easier to find reasons not to do something.
  - One interviewee was "*Amazed that most CEOs of pension funds are more scared of doing wrong than taking risk and moving the needle.*"
  - Another stated that "*The challenge with this industry is that 99% of people just want to follow. Trying to do things you believe in has very little upside in our industry. People who have jobs like I do just get comfortable and want to clip their annuity at the end of the day.*"
  - There was also a sense of the wider benefits in collaboration. For example, joining low carbon investing partnerships was seen by some interviewees as a good way to overcome barriers as others feel collective risk is being taken.

- **External pressure:** Our discussions indicated that external pressures from beneficiaries/members, employers, regulators, NGOs or the media to take action can be effective at overcoming behavioural barriers and helping to prioritise climate change internally across asset owners' executive functions.
  - On the flipside, public scrutiny can also increase risk aversion amongst some Board members and create a fear of going too far on an issue and getting it wrong. For example, one interviewee stated, "*I submitted a plan for low carbon investment and the board asked me what will*

I tell the journalists if I get this wrong"?

— Another interviewee also noted the role of external advisors, and how this can present a challenge if the consultants (for example) are not fully supportive of taking action on climate change. *"It is easy for anybody along the way that wants to sow seeds of doubt - consultants for instance can always come up with reasons not to do it"*.

Summary

The research found evidence that indicates the barriers to capital allocation to climate finance is more complicated than investors simply needing additional information, government policies or regulations to support such actions. There are a multitude of internal conditions that influence investor behaviour that warrant closer attention by investors themselves, as well as by policy makers and financial regulators.

The mental models that people utilise and default to will ultimately determine whether the finance sector will allocate capital to close the climate financing gap at the speed and scale that is required. Some of the internal barriers that have been identified include not connecting investment beliefs with a broader sense of purpose, feeling uncomfortable with complexity, conforming to peer group norms, failure to reflect on personal agency, fragmented organisational culture, tension between short- and long-term goals, and a fear of failure. A closer look at the mindsets of individuals inside financial institutions is therefore needed, to help unravel some of these complex internal drivers so that we can move towards a balanced and resilient global ecosystem that will benefit us all.

References

American Psychology Association (2009). Psychology and Global Climate Change: Addressing a Multi-faceted Phenomenon and Set of Challenges. Report of the American Psychological Association Task Force on the Interface Between Psychology and Global Climate Change. Available at: http://www.apa.org/science/about/publications/climate-change.aspx.

Carvalho, A. (2010). Climate change as a grand narrative. Journal of Science Communication, 09(04). https://doi.org/10.22323/2.09040303.

Daumas, L. (2023). Financial stability, stranded assets and the low-carbon transition – A critical review of the theoretical and applied literatures. Journal of Economic Surveys, 00, 1– 116. https://doi.org/10.1111/joes.12551

Farr, R.M. (1997). The new economic mind: The social psychology of economic behavior: A. Lewis, P. Webley, and A. Furnham (eds.), Hemel Hempstead, Harvester/Wheatsheaf.

Festinger, L., (1957). Social comparison theory. Selective Exposure Theory, 16, p.401.

Lewis, A. (2001). A focus group study of the motivation to invest: 'ethical/green' and 'ordinary' investors compared, Journal of Behavioral and Experimental Economics, 30, issue 4, p. 331-341.

Keynes, J.M. (1936). The General Theory of Employment, Interest and Money. Macmillan: London.

Schneider, F. W., Gruman, J. A., & Coutts, L. M. (2005). Applied social psychology: Understanding and addressing social and practical problems. Thousand Oaks, Calif: SAGE Publications.

Shiller, R.J. (2005). Behavioral Economics and Institutional Innovation. Southern Economic Journal, 72: 269-283. https://doi.org/10.1002/j.2325-8012.2005.tb00702.

Simon, H. A. (1982). Models of bounded rationality. Cambridge, MA: MIT Press. Rationality is bounded because there are limits to our thinking capacity, available information, and time.

Sunstein, C.R. (2018). The rise of behavioral economics: Richard Thaler's misbehaving. Journal of Behavioral Economics for Policy, Vol.2, No.1., pp.53-57. http://sabeconomics.org/wordpress/wp-content/uploads/JBEP-2-1-8.pdf

Thaler, R. H., Sunstein, C. R., & Balz, J. P. (2013). Choice architecture. In E. Shafir (Ed.), The behavioral foundations of public policy (pp. 428–439). Princeton University Press.

Tversky, A., & Kahneman, D. (1982). Judgment under uncertainty: Heuristics and biases. In D. Kahneman, P. Slovic, & A. Tversky (Eds.), Judgment under Uncertainty: Heuristics and Biases (pp. 3-20). Cambridge: Cambridge University Press. doi:10.1017/CBO9780511809477.002.

Van der Linden, S. (2017). Determinants and Measurement of Climate Change Risk Perception, Worry, and Concern. In book: Oxford Research Encyclopedia of Climate Science, Oxford University Press, editor M. Nisbett.

6. Capital allocation decisions through a sustainable mindset lens

> *"Despite major progress in recent years, more is required to build the right frameworks for the private sector to do what it does best: allocate capital to manage risks and seize opportunities."*
> Source: Carney (2020)

This chapter applies the sustainable mindset for finance framework to analyse the specific challenge of closing the climate financing gap. To set the scene for this discussion, the statement above by Mark Carney is a useful starting point, as it illustrates that even an industry thought leader assumes and reaffirms the belief that investors are very good at allocating capital, if only the system and the frameworks would allow them to do this properly when it comes to issues like sustainability and climate change. This assumption fails to consider the evidence of a well-documented and persistent misallocation of capital which raises questions about how well the current approach to capital allocation serves the needs of others (Banerjee and Moll (2010); He and Qi (2021); and Clayton and Schaab (2023). Certainly, when it comes to allocating capital to climate change, the persistent gap in the climate financing needs is indicative that capital is not flowing to where it is needed. As Kreibiehl et al (2022) noted in Chapter 15 of the IPCC AR6:

> *"There's no shortage of money globally: it is simply that it has yet to travel to where it's most needed."*
> Kreibiehl et al (2022)

We are therefore witness to a deeply ingrained bias within the financial sector to avoid looking at the allocation of capital process too closely, preferring to assume first and foremost that the 'right frameworks' need to be developed to fit into existing processes.

This call for the 'right frameworks' to support private sector capital allocation include conditions such as good governance, policy stability, market access, liquidity, and currency stability, all of which are valid and important pursuits (Carney, 2020). However, these are conditions that are prevalent and underpin all capital allocation decisions, they are not unique to climate finance. Furthermore, if we rely too heavily on the supporting conditions to only come from the external environment, we risk overlooking the importance of our own internal processes and mental models to mobilise capital. It might indeed be that change to both the external and internal conditions need to occur, although the external conditions dominate where the industry focuses its attention. So, given the importance of the problem that we collectively face with respect to climate change, we need to pay more attention to the internal barriers to correct this imbalance.

What if we asked the question differently, what if Mohammed agreed to go to the mountain? What if we stopped trying to move the mountain and we ourselves walk towards it? Would investors think about allocating capital to 'manage risks' and 'seize opportunities' to avert catastrophic climate change impacts differently? What would that look like? Is there a more expansive way to approach this challenge?

This is where the sustainable mindsets for finance framework comes into the picture. If indeed, the industry needs new frameworks to help it to allocate capital to where it is most needed, then the mindsets framework could be part of the armoury. It is not typical for investors to look inwards and ask the sort of questions that are suggested in the mindset framework, but if anything, that reaffirms why this is needed.

> When we encounter challenges or indeed find ourselves making assumptions that avoid looking at our own internal processes and mental models and focus only on the prevailing external conditions, can we pause to reflect and ask ourselves, is there another way to look at this issue? What am I assuming? What am I missing here?

The other notable consideration is the extent to which we can shift the focus of the finance sector from aligning with a certain climate pathway, to actions that will enable that pathway. For example, we have seen that international and high-profile networks such as the Glasgow Financial Alliance for Net Zero (GFANZ) have a stated intention to help mobilise capital and recognise the important role that the private sector plays in climate financing, yet the language and guidance used is still somewhat opaque. The recommendations and guidance for investors when developing their net zero plans refers to *"aligning the financial sector with the net-zero transition"* (GFANZ, 2022). The distinction between 'alignment with' (which is more passive) versus 'enabling' net zero has important ramifications.

Oxford English Dictionaries defines each term as follows:

- Alignment = a position of agreement or alliance
- Enabling = make something possible, operational; activate.

Consequently, enabling net zero and climate resilience sets a different intention to alignment, as enabling would mean that investors pro-actively allocate capital to support climate transition and adaptation activities to close the financing gap. Alignment with that outcome is, in comparison, a much more passive pursuit.

> As many investors have already set an intention to align with a net zero climate change pathway, can we ask what it would mean if we described our goal in terms of enabling this outcome? What would that mean? What would that look like in terms of how we think about capital allocation? How can we cultivate this mindset shift?

Applying the sustainable mindset for finance framework

The aim in developing a sustainable mindset framework for the finance sector (herein referred to as the 'mindset framework') was not to try to teach people how to think. No one can teach another person how to think. We can, however, offer ways to reconceptualise our existing understandings and perceptions of purpose and how we do things. We can start to approach challenges from a different perspective, to turn inwards and not only seek change from the external conditions; to open new ways to think and find creative solutions. The mindset framework is therefore intended to facilitate this process of internal enquiry, to understand how we feel, think, and behave as being relevant and important for addressing sustainability issues. A summary of the sustainable mindset framework for finance is presented in Figure 22. with further details provided in Chapter 3.

Figure 22. Highlights of the Sustainable Mindset for Finance Framework

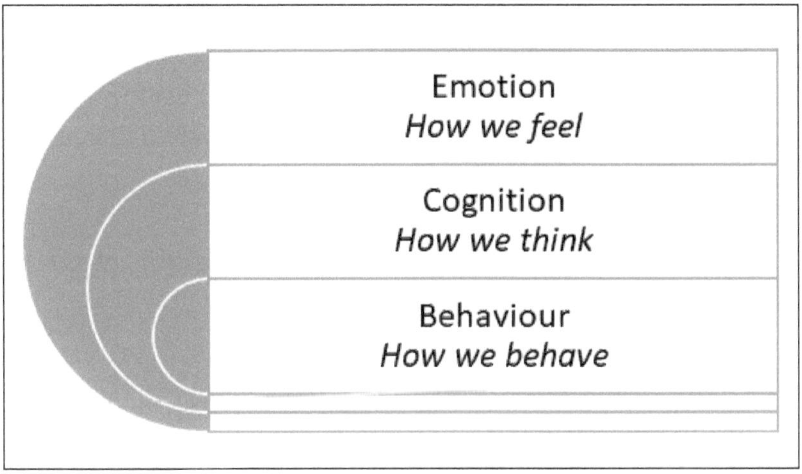

The mindset framework is relevant for financial institutions who are in the process of developing a sustainability policy, or already have some form of sustainability objective, policy, goal, or program of work in place, and are interested in exploring alternative ways to achieve these goals and manage any challenges that might arise.

It could be applied through a facilitated team setting or for individual contemplation, by simply thinking about each of the questions and issues and extending the enquiry further where needed, depending on what issues arise and where the greatest potential for development might be. It could also be included in part of an organisation's board, committee and staff training and development programs.

Industry standard setting agencies and financial regulators could also utilise the mindset framework, to encourage financial institutions to look at some of the internal barriers to achieving their sustainability goals and make efforts to address these. It could be embedded into the reporting and disclosure frameworks, for example, to acknowledge and encourage the important role that internal change and enquiry can play in creating a more sustainable, resilient, and prosperous financial system that serves the broader needs of everyone.

It is suggested that the application of the mindset framework be carried out in four stages as set out below:

1. Define the objective
2. Identify the barriers
3. Apply the mindset framework
4. Reflect and respond

Before we delve further into each of these areas and apply the mindset framework to the specific goal of increasing capital to close the climate financing gap, some of the overarching actions to guide this process are summarised in Figure 23. Just by simply reading through these suggested actions, pausing to think about what they could mean for you personally, and for your organisation, a change in perspective is invited.

Figure 23: Actions to guide the cultivation of a sustainable mindset

Ask different questions / ask questions differently.

Think about your long-term vision for how the world could be, and your role in creating that.

Think about what issues you are most passionate and/or concerned about.

Revisit core purpose – why the organisation exists and what this means for you.

Reference back to your beliefs and purpose as you make each decision.

Identify your sphere of influence and agency, how you can make an impact.

Before making any investment decisions, slow down, pause.

Take time out to connect to nature.

Listen to your inner wisdom.

Look after your well-being, and the well-being of others.

Reflect on the implications of your short-term decisions, check they align with your long-term vision.

Identify how your capital allocation decisions can shape your long-term vision.

Recognise the limits to linear thinking and economic growth and embrace the shift towards circularity and regeneration.

Explore how you can incorporate systems thinking into your investment frameworks.

Welcome diversity and seek alternative perspectives and sources.

Objectively analyse prevailing norms and assumptions.

Build a broader understanding of interconnections.

Take time to build skills to think beyond data.

Seek ways to be innovative and creative when challenges arise.

Read widely and be open to new research methods and techniques.

We will now apply these four stages and the guiding principles to see how it can work in practice. These stages are not intended to be prescriptive but are provided to support the process of enquiry into the internal dimensions that are not commonly considered in the context of the financial sector. The suggested questions and issues are provided to stimulate the imagination and search for an alternative way to think about the issues. They are not recommendations but serve as prompts for inner reflection and small group discussion.

Define the objective

The objective is to close the climate financing gap no later than 2030, by allocating private sector capital to where it is most needed.

Identify the barriers

The barriers that have been identified in achieving this objective have been explored in Chapters 5 and 6. In exploring other contexts and objectives, it would be helpful to unravel the potential barriers from multiple sources of information and enquiry that looks not only at the external conditions, but also at the inner dimensions.

In summary, the exploration of the dominant *external* barriers to climate finance that were identified in Chapter 5 from multiple sources and studies included:

1. Inconsistent government policy
2. Lack of information
3. Lack of common definitions
4. Lack of expertise
5. Liquidity barriers
6. Excessive deal pricing
7. Difficulty to access

In terms of the *internal* barriers to allocating capital to climate finance, the key factors that were identified and summarised in Chapter 6 included:

1. Disconnect from beliefs and broader purpose
2. Uncomfortable with complexity
3. Conforming to peer group
4. Failure to reflect on personal agency
5. Not embedded into culture
6. Tension between the short and long term
7. Fear of failure

It just so happens that the review identified 7 external and internal barriers to closing the financing gap, in practice you may discover more (or less) issues to the specific challenge that you have identified. We will now apply the mindset framework to look at these identified barriers through than lens to see if there are alternative ways that we can look at each of these challenges.

External barriers

This refers to the barriers that are about 'the other', rather than the self. We often think that a barrier can only be solved by someone or something else changing (e.g., new government policies, more corporate reporting) when in fact, we may also be able to address these issues by changing how we think about them. So even the way we perceive and respond to so-called external barriers reflect our mindset.

Inconsistent government policy

One of the most common explanations for the lack of capital allocation to climate finance from the perspective of the financial sector and institutional investors, is the prevailing inconsistency in government policies. This is the starting point for most interactions and dialogue between investors and governments. However, government policy is notoriously inconsistent across several dimensions, this need not be a reason to delay investing, it just means that policy uncertainty needs to be embedded into how climate-related assets are evaluated.

Given how far we have come in the climate discussions and commitments through the UNFCCC COP process, the direction of travel is clear. This means that in many cases, government policy refinement is a 'nice to have' rather than essential for fundamental change, as we all know and understand what is needed.

Alternative perspective:

It is possible that the extensive effort and focus on what governments need to do, is resulting in the financial sector not looking more closely at how it can address some of these barriers, and move towards being a co-creator in the transformation process?

Can I/we phase out the financing of thermal coal and fossil fuel assets from our financing activities, just as many investors have requested governments do?

Can I/we focus on financing companies and activities that are enabling a net zero by 2050 future, including in the primary markets to help build the industries that they rightly identify as being needed?

Can I/we play a role in building energy security by investing in the technologies and infrastructure that we identify as being needed?

Can I/we undertake analysis to define the sector goals and pathways for the transition as part of their investment and financial analysis processes, just as many investors have requested governments do?

Can I/we play a role in building demand for green products, including through offering new investment options and mandates to stakeholders?

Can I/we explore ways to invest in more pre-commercial technologies to accelerate the change process and underpin innovation?

Can I/we explore options for allocating more capital to green infrastructure assets in emerging market regions?

Can I/we consider what role I/we could play in financing

the adaptation needs of the global and local communities in which we are based?

These questions are not intended to deflect all the responsibility back to investors, but it is provided to widen the context for the discussions. If those actions by government are needed as defined by investors, what could investors themselves do differently (in addition to asking governments for greater action) to help combat some of these obstacles?

Lack of information

Another prominent explanation put forward by the finance sector as a barrier to climate finance is the lack of information. However, the volume and quality of information is only part of the story, the important consideration is how the information will be interpreted by investors, the mental models and framing for sense making of the data and information. Information is not a panacea. An alternative way to think about the perceived lack of information is provided below.

Alternative perspective:

Traditional economic theory posits that efficient capital allocation requires the right information, so that investors can make informed decisions and correctly price or value assets. So, we begin a large and earnest quest via the TCFD to gather more data, to develop frameworks, to spread the word of hope that more information will help us avoid misallocating capital in the face of climate change.

Five years later, we have a persistently wide climate

financing gap, and the misallocation of resources that we were concerned could happen due to a lack of information, is taking place right before our eyes. By not redirecting capital to where it is needed to combat climate change, investors are perpetuating the misallocation of resources even further and risking catastrophic climate outcomes.

Imperfect information need not be a reason to not invest in climate finance activities. All markets have a degree of imperfect information, that is what makes market work and indeed, is the condition that provides greater return potential for investors.

Is it possible that investors are overlooking the most important and obvious information that is right in front of them? The science of climate change, the economic costs of climate change, the regions and sectors that will be impacted, the industries of the future, technological pathways, policy pathways. There is a plethora of data and research, robust evidence, on all of these issues from credible sources.

Is the quest for more information an unintentional delay tactic, an avoidance strategy – or at best, an admission that there could be a need to build a deeper understanding of these issues?

Is there a risk of information overload?

What specific questions am I/we trying to answer with the information?

What additional information do I/we think is needed to change our capital allocation decisions?

How will I use this information?

These questions are not intended to suggest that data and

information is not important. Of course, it is vital as climate change and climate financing are complex issues. But clearly, we have over-estimated the importance of information alone in mobilising capital to climate finance activities. According to the TCFD, we have a lot of additional data and information being reported in the past five years, yet the financial flows to climate finance have not shifted.

We need to consider not only the type of information that investors say they need, but moreover how investors intend to use this information as part of the capital allocation decision making process. We need to get to the heart of the matter and not assume that more information will lead to the most efficient allocation of capital to protect the future health and resilience of our ecosystem.

Lack of common definitions

Another obstacle to capital allocation that the financial sector has spent a lot of time trying to solve over recent years is the lack of common definitions when it comes to classifying what is a climate mitigation / adaptation activity.

As Chapter 5 highlighted, there are several reasons why the taxonomy process could have very little impact on capital allocation flows into climate finance from the finance sector in the timeframe that is required. First, it takes considerable time to formulate and agree the definitions; second; there is a lack of common definitions across jurisdictions; and third, self-interest and corporate interference can result in the definitions being watered down.

With these caveats in mind, an alternative way to look at the apparent need for definitions to guide capital allocation decisions is provided.

Alternative perspective:

One of the fundamental reasons for establishing a sustainability taxonomy is to provide a common set of definitions on transition and adaptation activities. This could then be used for a variety of purposes, including to guide capital allocation decisions for financial institutions.

The process is a very slow and time intensive exercise and is only just commencing in some jurisdictions. The country-based approach that has emerged has resulted in a variety of different definitions and classifications in different jurisdictions, with the nuanced definitions reflecting local economic interests, rather than the scientific evidence on what is (or is not) a transition activity.

If we revisit one of the original goals behind the taxonomy process, which was to develop a common set of definitions to guide capital allocation decisions for financial institutions, might there be an alternative way to approach this challenge

that would be: a) less time intensive and hence quicker to impact on capital allocation decisions; b) based on rigorous science, and hence consistent across sectors and regions; and c) reported and measurable, to improve transparency.

As an alternative to waiting for a common taxonomy to inform investors as to what is (or is not) a transition or adaptation activity, can the scientific sources that are widely available be used as the basis to guide such decisions, right now?

What activities are the most contentious, and how can these be incorporated into internal investment processes?

Can the financing of climate transition and adaptation activities be included in investment policy guidelines now, and be updated regularly in response to new information and evidence (rather than waiting for a taxonomy)?

Once again, these questions are not designed to undermine the importance of the taxonomy process which has many benefits and may very well arrive at a suitable point in the future to guide capital allocation decisions. But given the urgency and present limitations with this process as it is unfolding, there are processes that investors could implement today that would deliver an immediate impact on both transparency and capital allocation decisions.

Lack of expertise

Several industry and academic studies that have attempted to unravel the challenges of mobilising capital into climate finance have identified a lack of expertise and knowledge as a possible barrier to action (OECD, 2014). With the plethora of research, industry reports, investment guides and so forth that are available, claiming not to have the expertise to act on climate change is potentially a breach of fiduciary duty. An alternative way to think about building capacity is provided below.

Alternative perspective:

To what extent do I/we leverage the existing skills of staff and investment teams to evaluate climate finance opportunities?

If expertise is lacking within our teams to undertake the analysis needed, am I/we accessing the appropriate resources and undertaking training to build the knowledge and capabilities that are required to make informed decisions on these matters?

Do I/we think about climate finance as an opportunity to innovate and keep abreast of global trends, or as a compliance or reporting activity?

What collaboration or partnership opportunities are available (or could be developed) that would help to build the experience and expertise that is needed?

Liquidity barriers

Another barrier to climate financing that often arises is the illiquid nature of the investment opportunities and the perceived lack of depth in the markets (including in developing markets) (OECD, 2021). The industry is pursuing some solutions to this through regulations, market reform and blended finance approaches. If we apply an exploratory and problem-solving mindset to this challenge, we may start to think about additional solutions related to redesign and innovation in terms of how we approach capital allocation decisions.

Alternative perspective:

Given the liquidity implications and capital constraints that financial institutions face, there is clearly a need for a system wide review of the 'rules of the game' that will enable financial institutions to increase their allocation of capital to climate finance opportunities in illiquid assets. The industry has rightly identified that this requires a review of financial regulations, collaboration between the public and private sector and DFIs, as well as blended finance structures.

In the interim, financial institutions and in particular institutional investors could consider how they can reorient their internal processes to prioritise the allocation of capital to climate finance opportunities versus other types of illiquid assets that they might consider. This could help to divert not only new fund inflows into climate finance activities, but it could also steer the redemptions of existing investments in illiquid assets into climate finance.

In addition, investors could consider building internal expertise and/or collaboration with others to leverage expertise in the industry such that they could invest more capital into primary and direct climate finance investments, compared to the more typical fund and third-party structures that many investors might utilise. Given the scale and urgency of the challenge at hand, a rethink of the tools available and how these might need to be redesigned is warranted.

Some questions to consider as part of this review process:

If liquidity thresholds are an obstacle to investing in climate finance, are there alternative vehicles, structures or partnerships that could be prioritised (or be built) that would allow more capital allocation to take place?

What proportion of existing illiquid asset allocation could be diverted towards climate finance activities as/when the investments mature, and the funds are redeemed?

What proportion of new fund inflows could immediately be diverted towards climate finance activities as/when the funds are received, with a particular focus on allocation to developing markets?

What new collaboration or partnership opportunities can be fostered to help provide access to the climate finance deals that might be available outside of existing networks and relationships?

Excessive deal pricing

Another factor that has been identified by some investors when considering capital allocation to climate finance opportunities is the excessive pricing of some of the deal flow. This is most likely a cyclical and/or temporary situation and is not universal across all types of assets and regions (Blanc-Brude and Amenc, 2022). This is not in itself a reason not to invest, it just requires a different way to think, as suggested below.

Alternative perspective:

As an alternative to making general assumptions about deal pricing for climate finance assets, can I/we take steps to prioritise and consider the pricing of opportunities on a case-by-case basis, as we do for other capital allocation decisions.

In addition, can I/we consider alternative ways to access the climate finance opportunities in addition to the more traditional modes of bonds and equities, such as primary market and direct investments.

Some questions to consider:

Have I/we prioritised the search for climate mitigation and adaptation assets in developed and developing markets?

Have the asset pricing models been adequately revised and tested to consider the fair value of assets under future climate scenarios and trajectories?

If there is a premium being paid for some climate mitigation assets, to what extent is that a fair reflection of the future trajectory of these assets compared to higher carbon counterparts, which may become stranded?

To what extent does the cost of runaway climate change justify any short-term price differential for climate mitigation or adaptation activities, to the extent that a differential exists?

How can I/we gain more visibility on project financing deal flow and pricing in relation to climate finance activities?

What networks, platforms and partnerships could be formed to facilitate this?

Difficulty to access

Difficulty in accessing the investment opportunities, especially in emerging markets, is another explanation sometimes put forward for the lack of capital allocation into climate finance (Carney, 2020). However, there are some well-considered frameworks and recommendations that have been developed by reputable sources to improve access to the opportunities (OECD, 2021). The question for investors going forward is therefore how to best use and leverage this body of knowledge and guidance, as access to opportunities is no longer a tenable rationale for failing to do so. Some questions to consider as part of this process are provided below.

> Some questions to consider:
>
> Am I utilising the broader networks needed to access opportunities in emerging and developing economies?
>
> What is stopping me?
>
> Have a looked at the opportunities?
>
> What did I find?
>
> Am I / my team energised to seek partnerships and build knowledge in this area?
>
> Have I defined what markets, assets, and regions I will focus my research efforts on?
>
> Can I think about the risks and opportunities in a different way when it comes to allocating capital to developing economies, where the financing needs are greatest?

Internal barriers

This refers to the barriers that are about what I/my organisation can change, about how we feel, think, and behave. These are much less prevalent in the industry-wide literature, although there is a raft of academic research on the psychological barriers to climate action that we can draw from in different contexts (APA, 2009; Van der Linden, 2017; Carney, 2015; Tversky & Kahneman, 1982;

Thaler, Sunstein & Balz, 2013; Schneider, Gruman & Coutts, 2005; and Colgan, 2018). In terms of the specific context of climate change and investor behaviour, Chapter 6 summarised research on investor behaviour (ClimateWorks, 2019) that identified some insights for considering the mindset shift that is needed. The key findings from that review will now be explored, with some prompts and questions to support a mindset shift.

Disconnect from beliefs and broader purpose

Chapter 6 presented evidence of a disconnect between climate change, investment beliefs and a broader sense of purpose (ClimateWorks, 2019). More specifically, while climate change was seen as a "top 5" issue by some investors, others feel that there are multiple and "equally pressing" issues that also need to be addressed, suggesting that climate change can wait. The prevalence of "knowing and not knowing" (Norgaard, 2006) produces cognitive dissonance and a level of internal conflict and discomfort. Yes, there is general acknowledgment of climate change as a systemic risk, but in practice at the day-to-day level, there is a degree of separation from the issue in terms of decisions that are made.

This broader sense of purpose needs to explore not only the goal of maximising financial returns, as that is the outcome of *what* you do, not *why* you do it. Why you do what you do, your broader purpose, the legacy you want to leave, the imprint you make on how the capital market functions and your ability to serve the needs of others and allocate capital to where it is most needed.

Boards, investment committees and everyone involved in this

process need to spend time exploring how they feel about any arbitrary lines that have been drawn in the sand, as automatic responses are often based on assumptions that have not been challenged or deeply explored.

Drawing from the mindset framework, some questions to consider bringing a greater connection between beliefs, purpose and climate finance are suggested below.

> It is inconsistent to believe that climate change is a major systemic risk, and at the same time relegate it to the not so important category, it cannot be both. Either the beliefs are not very deeply held, or there is a disconnect that needs to be unravelled. It may be that the broader sense of purpose has not been fully developed or defined. This disconnect is not something that an external solution can address, it needs to come from the inside.
>
> What is needed is a deeper understanding and connection between investor's knowledge about climate change and the financing needs, with their beliefs and broader sense of purpose.
>
> What is often missing from discussions about beliefs and purpose is an explicit focus on the link between capital allocation decisions and creating real-world outcomes. In other words, a shift in perspective from being a *responder* to the external conditions that prevail, to one that is a co-creator of a more sustainable future.
>
> A lower level of conviction or weaker beliefs might stop short of making these connections, with some relegating the connection to real world impact to the narrower remit of 'impact' investing, rather than seeing that every investment decision has a real-world impact.

Every investor with some influence over capital allocation decisions therefore needs to think about and articulate the reason why the financial institution that they work for exists, who it serves and what needs it fulfills, what that means to them personally, and how climate finance is related to fulfilling this purpose.

Some questions to consider as part of this process, both at the individual and organisational level:

Do I/we believe that a more secure, safer, and prosperous world will be beneficial for our stakeholders and the people whose needs we are serving?

Do I believe that I can help to create that world through my capital allocation decisions?

Where is capital most needed to provide a secure, safe and prosperous world now and into the future?

Am I aware of the climate financing gap?

How concerned am I about this?

How can I accelerate how much capital is allocated to these areas with the urgency that is required?

Is this a priority for me / for our organisation?

Why or why not?

Before I look at what others need to do (governments, companies) have I fully explored what I can do?

What will happen if I prioritise the allocation of capital to close this gap?

What do I need to do to prioritise this pursuit?

What do I think will happen if I don't do this?

Uncomfortable with complexity

The complexity of responding to the climate change challenge can make some investors feel uncomfortable, as the issues may not easily fit into existing investment frameworks (ClimateWorks, 2019). There is a resistance to changing existing frameworks, as it takes time and energy, and the motivation can be lacking. Scenario analysis has emerged to help think about complexity whilst maintaining existing capital allocation frameworks. The challenge of course is that interpreting the outputs from scenario analysis and linking this to the investment frameworks still requires a skillset that might be lacking, that holds back adapting capital allocation in response to the scenario analysis pathways.

No amount of data, tools or standards will (in itself) address specifically this feeling of being uncomfortable with complexity. This is a barrier related to how people respond and deal with complexity and the time, effort and motivation that is needed to review existing frameworks and respond. Investment committees can spend considerable time debating the outputs from climate scenario pathways but still feel uncomfortable about linking this analysis to their capital allocation decisions (ClimateWorks, 2019).

It is impossible to genuinely pursue the goal of closing the climate financing gap unless the people involved in capital allocation decisions are willing to explore and unravel why they feel uncomfortable with complexity, what they are afraid of in reflecting scenario analysis into capital allocation decisions, and if there is an alternative way for them to think about and approach these issues. Some questions are provided below to prompt and guide such discussions.

> The financial sector depends heavily on 'data' to justify its capital allocation decisions, even though this has its shortcomings; the selection of data is subjective and past events are not accurate predictions of the future (as every prospectus of a financial institution explains). When future events are highly complex and unprecedented, such as climate change, then it is very limiting to rely too heavily on historical time series to guide decisions.
>
> The complexities of climate change require us, as investors, to build an understanding of the uncertainties, exercise our judgement, and seek divergent perspectives to guide capital allocation decisions. Scenario analysis is a useful tool in this regard, but we need to focus our attention on the 'so what' and adapt capital allocation frameworks to incorporate such analysis.
>
> Closing the climate financing gap is part of our broader sense of purpose, and we understand that how we allocate capital can help to shape the mitigation and adaptation pathways, which is a step beyond alignment (that may have been the focus in the past).
>
> A system thinking approach would help to counteract these tendencies, as investors would start with a recognition that an assessment of future risks requires consideration of the dynamic

interactions within complex systems, where there may not be historical time series or past events to predict outcomes.

It is essential that investors develop the skills to think beyond data and be able to make well considered and well-informed decisions about the future. The sources and perspectives might be different to those that they are used to, new frameworks and skills might be needed to think more broadly, but this needn't be a reason to delay or avoid cultivating a deeper understanding to enrich investment decisions. Qualitative research techniques can be utilised more in supporting such decisions.

Some questions to consider as part of this process:

At the organisation wide level, can we prioritise the allocation of capital to climate finance activities?

Are we willing to spend the time and energy that is required to seek these opportunities?

Do we need to define the asset classes or risk factors differently?

Do we need to modify our capital allocation process to prioritise climate finance?

If so, in what way?

Are we willing to do this?

At the ***individual*** level, have I got the networks, knowledge, and capabilities to make informed assessments on climate mitigation and adaptation assets?

If not, can I build these connections and capabilities?

When I am deciding to invest in one asset versus another, have I explicitly considered if the activity of the company or asset will contribute to mitigating or adapting to climate change?

How much have I relied on historical data to identify the characteristic of assets that will perform well in the future in view of climate change?

Have I explored alternative sources of information and research techniques including qualitative research, and looked beyond the data?

Have I paused to consider and identify the uncertainties that cannot be explained or understood through data, but require me to form a judgement?

Am I comfortable making such judgments?

If not, what do I need to do to feel more comfortable in doing so?

Conforming to industry norms

There is evidence to suggest that some investors do not think their peers are taking strong action on climate change in terms of capital allocation, and that the industry's focus is primarily on engagement with policy makers and investee companies (ClimateWorks, 2019). This can undermine the motivation to go beyond what others are doing and hold back capital allocation to climate finance, as investors have a strong urge to conform to the norms of the industry, especially when it comes to issues that challenge the status quo (Guyatt. 2006).

At a deeper level, the tendency to conform to the behaviour of peers is also connected to a tendency to adhere to the rules of the game, in terms of how the market functions and the paradigms that prevail. That means that investors can internalise the prevailing market norms, embedded assumptions and existing paradigms, and reaffirm the strength of these in terms of how they invest and their willingness (or not) to invest capital to where it is most needed.

One of these dominant paradigms is the pursuit of infinite GDP growth in a world of finite resources. As discussed in Chapter 3, almost everyone in finance has been trained and educated to believe that maximising GDP growth is a valid pursuit and, similarly, the goal of maximising short term returns on investment is consistent with that quest. However, there is growing realisation that the planetary boundaries place a limit to how much economic growth we can sustain, and that investment returns can be redirected towards activities that pursue circularity and regeneration of finite resources, as opposed to infinite GDP growth (Wahl, 2016; Fullerton, 2015).

This realisation also invites a wider perspective on our own health and connection with nature, and how that can give rise to a greater awareness of the impact of capital allocation decisions on the health and resilience of the broader ecosystem. As we are in a process of transition with emerging paradigms not yet fully internalised into the 'rules of the game', the tendency for investors to conform to prevailing norms is being destabilised, but not yet replaced.

Some financial institutions are aware of the need for a new economic approach and see the merit of systems thinking, the circular economy and regeneration economics, however, this awareness is not yet widely embedded into capital allocation frameworks.

Systems thinking would guide people towards pro-actively finding ways to contribute to financing activities that support a reduction in consumption and waste, and an increase in recycling and re-using of materials, as well as activities that support the regeneration of the ecosystem.

As we are in a stage of profound change and paradigm shift, investors that seek a greater connection between their beliefs, broader sense of purpose and capital allocation decisions can practice some techniques to help them become more aware of the paradigms and assumptions that they are conforming to, become more willing to question and debate the efficacy of these conventions, and more open to resisting those that are no longer helpful.

Some questions to consider as part of this process:

At the ***organisational / team*** level, can we pause to recognise when a capital allocation decision might be driven by external pressures and adherence to prevailing norms and try to formulate an alternative response?

When making asset allocation decisions, have we considered what would happen to this asset if economic growth was no longer a viable pursuit or outcome?

How resilient would the asset be in a circular economy, where finite resources reward behaviours, products and services that minimise consumption, resource usage and waste and encourage recycling and regeneration?

What other assets can we consider that would thrive in a circular economy where regeneration proliferated?

Failure to reflect on agency

Evidence suggests that some investors are more willing to focus on changing the behaviour or others (governments, companies, regulators) and are less willing to look internally at their own agency and what they could do differently in terms of capital allocation (ClimateWorks, 2019). While engagement with policy makers and companies is a strong part of investor's armoury to exercise their influence in those spheres, the link between investor's agency and capital allocation decisions can often be overlooked or considered 'too difficult' to address.

This lack of agency relates directly to the broader sense of purpose and beliefs of each investor and organisation, as some may feel that it is the role of governments to solve problems such as how to close the climate financing gap; that investors are merely responding to the conditions that exist and cannot alter their own frameworks to pursue such a goal. Some might believe that climate financing could have negative implications for short term performance, or they are unsure and afraid that this could be the outcome.

A broader sense of purpose that seeks to serve others and allocate capital to where it is most needed would invite a different perspective and focus on this quest; engaging with governments to create more supportive conditions but also pro-actively steering capital towards the common goal of closing the climate financing gap, by investigating, creating and investing in the opportunities to allocate capital to where it is most needed.

It is possible that the debate about divesting from fossil fuels has obscured the focus of attention on where the mitigation and adaptation capital is needed most. With a sustainable mindset, lower allocation to assets and activities that contribute to the climate change problem, and higher allocation to those assets that provide solutions would naturally occur. What is missing is a wider recognition and utilisation of the financial sector's agency in terms of how capital is allocated, and how that can specifically help to close the climate financing gap for a safer and more resilient future for all. When the broader sense of purpose and agency are in alignment, then capital will flow to where it is most needed. We don't need to wait for more data and standards to help us form these connections, we can do this right now by exercising our agency to its full potential.

In the context of closing the climate financing gap, consider how capital allocation decisions impact on real-world outcomes and reflect on how that influence can be utilised.

> Some questions to consider as part of this process:
>
> Have I identified how I can exercise my influence in terms of how capital is allocated, in particular, how I/we can help to close the climate financing gap?

Can I pause to consider how each capital allocation decision or action feels before proceeding?

Does the decision help to close the climate financing gap?

Have I checked back to my beliefs and broader sense of purpose to see how the investment aligns with that?

Do I feel comfort, discomfort, or something else?

As I pause to reflect, is there a feeling of conflict, or does the decision feel 'right'?

Could I make a different capital allocation decision, that would reduce the feeling of conflict and better align with my broader sense of purpose?

Are there other asset classes or investments that would contribute to closing the climate financing gap that I/we can consider?

Not embedded into culture

Climate change and sustainability issues have emerged as issues of high importance within the finance sector, although shortage of resources and cultural change can slow down progress. When there is a specialist team of people that sit outside the mainframe of an organisation, there is often an expectation that these issues are their responsibility, and the rest of the organisation can carry on with its day-to-day processes (ClimateWorks, 2019).

This can and is resulting in increased levels of burnout inside the financial sector, as subject specialists are not only in short supply, but they are not necessarily organisational change management experts and hence may not have the skills or experience to turn around an entire organisation. This is not only an unhealthy and unsustainable situation for the people that are at risk of burn out, but it is also harmful for the culture of the organisation and industry more broadly. We all need to feel a sense of connection and shared responsibility to address the collective challenges that we face.

What this means in terms of capital allocation decisions is that a disconnect can exist inside organisations between the people who are the subject specialists, and the people who are responsible for the capital allocation decisions. Very rarely are the two functions and responsibilities inside a financial institution integrated (despite some best efforts to do so). Consequently, while the specialists may be preparing Board papers and working with investment teams to encourage them to look at climate finance opportunities, it is often considered to be a secondary issue to the main business of investing capital. The language between the teams is different, their expertise, the information, and models that they are familiar with and hence rely on are very different. The specialist may have internalised a greater sense of purpose, but people responsible for capital allocation decisions may not have done so (ClimateWorks, 2019).

All these challenges are not insurmountable and indeed are quite easily resolved if the executive, management, and staff of an organisation is willing to explore options to change the culture and bring the different teams and perspectives closer together. Some questions to consider as part of this process are provided below.

If an organisation is genuine about wanting to achieve sustainable outcomes and would like the culture of the organisation to reflect that pursuit, then attention needs to be given to align the intrinsic and extrinsic motivations of its people, across and within teams.

In a situation where investors feel energised about allocating capital to climate finance activities, and the culture of the organisation and behaviour of others reinforce that pursuit, then there will be a greater sense of harmony internally and within the organisation and culture more broadly.

Investors in that situation are more likely to turn their mind towards any challenges or obstacles in regard to capital allocation with curiosity and creativity to problem solve, rather than become disengaged or reactive.

At an organisational level, this might include reviewing the design of HR policies, hiring and performance review processes, training and education programs and other initiatives that impact on organisational culture.

Each person needs to feel responsible for achieving the organisation's broader sense of purpose, not only the subject specialists.

Everyone needs to be encouraged and supported to step back and think about what these issues mean to them, and how they can engage in the process, such that the effort comes from a place of internal motivation and inspiration and is not perceived to be imposed on them by others (or a compliance obligation).

In terms of closing the climate financing gap, if an organisation wants to contribute to closing the gap, then each person in the relevant committee/management and investment teams with influence over these decisions need to feel that this is a shared goal.

To inspire and motivate people to act, organisations can encourage innovation and new ways to identify, analyse and invest in the climate mitigation and adaptation opportunities.

Some possible questions to consider for each person with responsibility or influence over capital allocation decisions:

Have I identified and thought about what the climate finance needs are and how I might be able to invest in some of these?

What new approaches have I developed and implemented to identify, analyse, and invest in climate finance opportunities?

If I find myself getting stuck on what assets to avoid rather than imagining the industries of the future, can I consider what assets will likely thrive in a circular economy where regeneration proliferates?

If I find myself expecting that others will take care of these issues, can I pause to reflect on what I can do?

If I encounter challenges or conflicting signals when considering climate finance opportunities, do I look for solutions to these or think of different ways to tackle the issue?

If investing in these opportunities requires new skills, partnerships, or expertise beyond my current purview, do I look for ways to build these?

Have I found innovative ways to mitigate the potential risks that I previously might have considered to be unsurmountable to warrant investment?

Tension between the short and long term

The tension between the short and long-term horizons is a subject that often arises in the context of climate change. Research on investor behaviour indicates there can be a recognition that climate change exists and is a systemic risk, although there is a perceived tension between short term behaviour and long-term goals related to climate change (ClimateWorks, 2019). The important point to note here is that this is a perception and not necessarily reality.

The mindset framework showed that if our short-term decisions are consistent with our long-term vision, then this perceived tension is reduced as there will be greater alignment between what we do on a day-to-day basis and our long-term goals. Because our brains are wired to be rewarded by short term outcomes, it is more helpful to think about ways to ensure that these rewards and outcomes are in alignment with the longer-term pursuit (in this case, closing the climate financing gap), than trying to stop people from seeking short term rewards.

In terms of the practical implications for closing the climate financing gap, it is important that when we aspire to allocate capital to climate finance and shift the investment horizon to the long-term, that we recognise that this is as much about internal alignment with that goal as it is about our time horizon.

This means we need to create a vision for the future and imagine our role in achieving that outcome and use that as a guide for our short-term decisions.

Some questions to consider for aligning short term decisions with our long-term vision include:

How would I like the world to be in 10 years from now?

How can I help to create that world through how I allocate capital?

Is each investment decision enabling that vision?

What time horizon have I considered as part of my investment due diligence?

What impact will the investment have on future generations and the natural world?

Am I contributing to a more sustainable future with this investment?

Am I comfortable that my shorter-term capital allocation decisions reflect my longer-term vision?

Fear of failure

Some investors feel that the high level of uncertainty in evaluating climate change impacts makes it riskier to base investment decisions on, as it will also be harder to justify to others if it goes wrong (ClimateWorks, 2019). This can reaffirm the status quo and slow down innovation.

The mindset framework suggested that positive emotions that reward and stimulate actions could help to offset such fears. For example, when we take time to cultivate a systems perspective and a greater alignment between our actions and sense of purpose, then we are more likely to feel motivated and inspired to find innovative solutions to any challenges that arise. Practices such as pausing to reflect on these fears, reconnecting to the long-term vision for the future and connecting with nature and others could help to generate positive emotions and dampen down any fear of failure that might arise.

> Emotion can at times undermine our climate change actions, as fear of failure can lead to resistance. However, it can also be a powerful motivator and part of the mindset change process if it is recognised and harnessed in the right way. This process starts with cultivating emotional intelligence which includes increased self-awareness, self-regulation, motivation, empathy, and social skills, to help people and organisations adapt and change.
>
> Some questions to consider as part of this process:
>
> Do I feel comfortable that I could justify the decision to others?
>
> Why, or why not?
>
> Can I identify the key uncertainties and consider other perspectives on these?

Are there other sources of information or expertise I could draw from?

Have I paused to reflect on the wider consequences of this investment for the environment or communities that might be adversely impacted?

How do I feel about those potential impacts?

Is the investment in alignment with my long-term vision for the future and the role that I want to play in achieving that?

Reflect and respond

The final suggested stage of the process is to reflect and respond to the issues that arose as part of the internal enquiry, at the individual, team, and organisational level.

Some of the questions to consider at this stage might include: Was there a strong sense of resistance to some of the ideas or questions that arose during the process? What were these? Can they be examined further, perhaps by seeking views from others?

What were the topics that people felt the most passionate and excited about, where ideas started to flow, and people felt a sense of knowing what to do?

How can these areas be harnessed and incorporated into the capital allocation frameworks?

Were there any people in the team who emerged as potential leaders/champions of these insights for further development?

Would a process for ongoing review and reflection be helpful? Can you summarise the key learnings and next steps from here?

Summary

It is not typical for investors to look inwards and ask the sort of questions that are suggested in the application of the mindset framework, but if anything, that reaffirms why this is needed. Many of the barriers that stand in our way to allocate capital to close the financing gap are 'mind-made' and are therefore not unsurmountable or dependent on external conditions.

To explore these mind-made barriers, the mindset framework has been applied to consider how institutional investors can approach the specific goal of closing the climate financing gap through a process of inner enquiry. The four-step process included defining the goal, identifying the internal and external barriers to achieving that goal, applying the mindset framework to each of these barriers to consider alternative perspectives, and reflecting on what was learnt and next steps.

Up to now, the industry has been largely focused on changing the external conditions to mobilise capital, such as inconsistent government policy, lack of information, definitions and standards, lack of expertise, liquidity barriers, excessive deal pricing and difficulty in accessing the opportunities. But when we examined each of these barriers, we saw that these challenges might be best described as transitory, and not dissimilar to any market shift or new emerging paradigm. The question is whether the industry is willing to acknowledge that there is never certainty regarding the outcome when making decisions on any investment issue, so how we approach the financing of climate change mitigation and adaptation is more about how willing we are to use our wisdom and judgement to interpret the information, tools, skills, and frameworks that are already available to support those decisions.

That is where the inner dimensions come into play, as the lack of capital allocation to climate financing is as much about our mental models, with mind-made obstacles such as not connecting our beliefs with a broader sense of purpose, feeling uncomfortable with complexity, conforming to peer group norms, failure to reflect on our personal agency, fragmented organisational culture, tension between short- and long-term goals, and a fear of failure.

In addition, what is often missing from discussions around capital allocation to climate finance is an explicit focus on the link between capital allocation decisions and creating real-world outcomes. In other words, a shift in perspective to embrace systems thinking and recognise interdependencies; from being a responder to the external conditions that prevail, to one that is a co-creator of a more sustainable future.

By applying the mindset framework to this challenge, we illustrated that if investors can envision the future and imagine the role they want to play in realising that future, then their short-term decisions will be more aligned with that long-term pursuit. When there is a sense of agency and intrinsic motivation to act, then a creative and innovative response is more likely to follow when challenges or problems arise. There will be a greater level of awareness and willingness to challenge dominant assumptions and paradigms that are inconsistent with this vision.

Boards, investment committees and everyone involved in the capital allocation process inside financial institutions will therefore benefit from spending time identifying and exploring how they feel about any arbitrary lines that have been drawn in the sand, as automatic responses are often based on assumptions or patterns of behaviour that have not been challenged or deeply explored.

References

American Psychology Association. (2009). Psychology and Global Climate Change: Addressing a Multi-faceted Phenomenon and Set of Challenges. Report of the American Psychological Association Task Force on the Interface Between Psychology and Global Climate Change. Available at: http://www.apa.org/science/about/publications/climate-change.aspx.

Banerjee, A.V., and Moll, B. (2010). Why Does Misallocation Persist? American Economic Journal: Macroeconomics, 2 (1): 189-206.

Blanc-Brude, F., and Amenc, F. (2022). The Pricing of Green Infrastructure. Published by EDHEC Infrastructure & Private Assets Research Institute. Available: https://edhec.infrastructure.institute/paper/the-pricing-of-green-infrastructure/

Carney, M. (2015). BIS central bankers' speeches Mark Carney: Breaking the tragedy of the horizon -climate change and financial stability. Available at: https://www.bis.org/review/r151009a.pdf.

Carney, M. (2020). Building a financial system for net zero, Priorities for private finance for COP26. UN Special Envoy for Climate Action and Finance and the Prime Minister's Finance Adviser for COP26

Clayton, C., and Schaab, A. (2023). Regulation with Externalities and Misallocation in General Equilibrium. Toulouse School of Economics, Working Paper no.1445. https://www.tse-fr.eu/sites/default/files/TSE/documents/doc/wp/2023/wp_tse_1445.pdf

ClimateWorks. (2019). Institutional Investors and the Behavioral Barriers to Taking Action on Climate Change. A research project authored by Guyatt, D., and Poulter, J. Published by ClimateWorks Foundation. https://www.climateworks.org/wp-content/uploads/2019/10/Institutional_Investors__BehavioralBarriers_to_TakingAction_on_ClimateChange_101619.pdf

Colgan, J. (2018). The Market is Valuing Climate Risk All Wrong. Global Policy Journal. Available at: https://www.globalpolicyjournal.com/blog/06/07/2018/market-valuing-climate-risk-all-wrong.

Fullerton, J. (2015). Regenerative Capitalism. Address at Yale University's Center for Business and the Environment.

Glasgow Financial Alliance for Net Zero. (2022). Financial institution net-zero transition plans: fundamentals, recommendations and guidance. Published by GFANZ. Available at: https://assets.bbhub.io/company/sites/63/2022/09/Recommendations-and-Guidance-on-Financial-Institution-Net-zero-Transition-Plans-November-2022.pdf.

Guyatt, D. (2006). Identifying and Overcoming Behavioural Impediments to Long Term Responsible Investment: A Focus on UK Institutional Investors. PhD dissertation. Available at SSRN: https://ssrn.com/abstract=1911821 or http://dx.doi.org/10.2139/ssrn.1911821.

He, L.Y., and Qi, X.F. (2021). Resource Misallocation and Energy-Related Pollution. International Journal of Environmental Research and Public Health, 18(10), p.5158. doi:https://doi.org/10.3390/ijerph18105158.

Kreibiehl, S., T. Yong Jung, S. Battiston, P. E. Carvajal, C. Clapp, D. Dasgupta, N. Dube, R. Jachnik, K. Morita, N. Samargandi, M. Williams. (2022). Investment and finance. In IPCC, 2022: Climate Change 2022: Mitigation of Climate Change. Contribution of Working Group III to the Sixth Assessment Report of the Intergovernmental Panel on Climate Change [P.R. Shukla, J. Skea, R. Slade, A. Al Khourdajie, R. van Diemen, D. McCollum, M. Pathak, S. Some, P. Vyas, R. Fradera, M. Belkacemi, A. Hasija, G. Lisboa, S. Luz, J. Malley, (eds.)]. Cambridge University Press, Cambridge, UK and New York, NY, USA. doi: 10.1017/9781009157926.017

Norgaard, K. M. (2006). We Don't Really Want to Know. Environmental Justice and Socially Organized Denial of Global

Warming in Norway. Organization & Environment, 19(3), 347–370. https://doi.org/10.1177/1086026606292571

OECD. (2014). Financing climate change action: policy perspectives. Available at: https://www.oecd.org/env/cc/Financing-climate-change-action-policy-perspectives.pdf.

OECD. (2021). De-risking institutional investment in green infrastructure: 2021 progress update. OECD Environment Policy Papers, No. 28, OECD Publishing, Paris, https://doi.org/10.1787/357c027e-en.

Principles for Responsible Investment. (2022). Closing the funding gap: The case for ESG incorporation and sustainability outcomes in emerging markets. Published by the PRI. Available at: https://www.unpri.org/sustainable-development-goals/closing-the-funding-gap-the-case-for-esg-incorporation-and-sustainability-outcomes-in-emerging-markets/9430.article.

Schneider, F. W., Gruman, J. A., & Coutts, L. M. (2005). Applied social psychology: Understanding and addressing social and practical problems. Thousand Oaks, Calif: SAGE Publications.

Thaler, R. H., Sunstein, C. R., & Balz, J. P. (2013). Choice architecture. In E. Shafir (Ed.), The behavioral foundations of public policy (pp. 428–439). Princeton University Press.

Tversky, A., & Kahneman, D. (1982). Judgment under uncertainty: Heuristics and biases. In D. Kahneman, P. Slovic, & A. Tversky (Eds.), Judgment under Uncertainty: Heuristics and Biases (pp. 3-20). Cambridge: Cambridge University Press. doi:10.1017/CBO9780511809477.002.

Van der Linden, S,. (2017). Determinants and Measurement of Climate Change Risk Perception, Worry, and Concern. In book: Oxford Research Encyclopedia of Climate Science, Oxford University Press, editor M. Nisbett.

Wahl, D.C. (2016). Designing Regenerative Cultures. Triarchy Press, Axminster, England.

7. Conclusion

Despite hundreds of financial institutions with trillions of dollars of assets under management having committed to support the attainment of Net Zero by 2050 and climate resilience, the data shows that the capital allocation to climate financing activities by the private sector remains extremely low as a proportion of the capital that is available. The climate financing gap remains wide and persistent, and it is widely agreed that there is an urgent need to close this gap in the decade that we are currently in to avoid dangerous and catastrophic outcomes in the future.

At the industry wide and regulatory level, proponents of investor action tend to focus their efforts on creating the most conducive external conditions to support capital allocation to climate financing, such as reviewing government policies, developing regulatory guidance, best practice processes, improving reporting, industry standards, taxonomies, data, tools and metrics in the hope that data and information will propel investors to allocate capital to where it is most needed. Despite these efforts, the financing gap remains wide, and the clock is ticking.

We need to look for alternative explanations and ways to close this gap with the sense of urgency that the evidence warrants. We need to look at the mindset of the people working inside the financial sector, and the broader culture of the industry. We need to question the assumptions, the dominant paradigms and the industry norms that have prevailed for the past decades. We need a collective and individual mindset shift.

When we bring greater awareness and focus on the inner dimensions of the people who work inside the financial sector - and those that are connected to and oversee the sector - then we can build an environment where the urge to take action comes not only from external conditions, but is also a reflection of our how we think about issues, how we process information, what motivates us, and hence how we behave.

In developing a sustainable mindset for finance, we saw evidence to illustrate the limits of neoclassical thinking in understanding human behaviour and decision making under uncertainty. Evidence of misallocation of resources is well documented and persistent, yet we fail to question the basis upon which such decisions are made. We are witness to a deeply ingrained bias within the financial sector to avoid looking at the allocation of capital process too closely, preferring to assume first and foremost that the right conditions need to be developed to fit into existing processes.

If we rely too heavily on the supporting conditions to only come from the external environment, we risk overlooking the importance of our own internal processes and mental models to mobilise capital to where it is most needed. It might indeed be that change to both the external and internal conditions need to occur, although the external conditions dominate where the industry focuses its attention. So, given the importance of the problem that we collectively face with respect to climate change and sustainable development, we need to pay more attention to the internal barriers to correct this imbalance.
This is where the sustainable mindset for finance framework comes into the picture. If indeed, the industry needs new frameworks to

help it to allocate capital to where it is most needed, then the mindset framework could be part of the armoury. It is not typical for investors to look inwards and ask the sort of questions that are suggested in the mindset framework, but if anything, that reaffirms why this is needed.

In developing a sustainable mindset for finance framework, we explored evidence showing that emotions are more than biases that need to be corrected, they are part of the human condition and can be a powerful force for change if harnessed in the right way. We also saw that mindfulness and inner wisdom can help to guide the internalisation of a broader sense of purpose, a deeper realisation and connection to our beliefs and greater alignment between our short-term decisions and long-term vision, a broader understanding of the interlinkages and impact our decisions have on real world outcomes through systems thinking, and the courage to resist conventions and seek innovative solutions when challenges arise.

This means that people working inside the financial sector need to internalise systems thinking into their mental models and how they make investment decisions. A systems thinker would ask themselves how their decisions, and their role, can reflect the planetary boundaries and limits that are being tested, and allocate capital in a way that would not only stop exacerbating these imbalances, but would pro-actively pursue investments that can regenerate the system. A systems thinker would not assume or hope that someone else will do something, they see the bigger picture and their role within that, and they act.

When we think about fostering a long-term, sustainable mindset, we need to pause to consider what motivate us, what makes us feel inspired, creative, and passionate. When we connect that to our day-to-day decisions, then our short-term actions will be in alignment with our longer-term goals. This means that if an organisation is serious and genuine about wanting to achieve sustainable outcomes and would like to encourage a long-term mindset, then more attention needs to be given to support the alignment of intrinsic and extrinsic motivations of its people. We need to create a workplace and industry culture that embodies sustainability into how it thinks and behaves. If we do this, we will find that we will naturally give more regard to our own health, to the health of others and ultimately, to the health and sustainability of the entire ecosystem.

The framework calls upon the financial sector to engage in the process of learning and inner enquiry, to consider sustainability issues from a different perspective and to ask different questions of themselves at a more personal level. It is not a new rulebook for people to follow, or a new mantra to repeat. Rather, it is a framework to support the process of internal enquiry that could enable a more rapid acceleration of actions that support sustainable outcomes, simply by taking the time to look at how we think.

Annexure A

Survey on investor behaviour and climate change

Survey that was conducted as part of a study on Institutional Investors and the Behavioural Barriers to Taking Action on Climate Change, funded by ClimateWorks Foundation (ClimateWorks, 2019).

1. What type of organisation do you work for?

2. What best describes your role?

3. In what region are you based?

4. What is your age?

5. What is your gender?

6. To what extent do you agree or disagree with the following statements on climate change? (5-point scale, strongly agree to strongly disagree)

- It is a systemic risk that needs to be urgently addressed
- Taking action now will reduce future costs
- It provides new opportunities for investors
- It is too far into the future to assess
- There is little that investors can realistically do
- There are more pressing issues to address

7. In your opinion, how easy or difficult is it to incorporate climate change into existing investment frameworks?

8. To what extent do you believe that climate change is being addressed by other investors (including your peers)?

9. In your opinion, how easy or difficult is it to adopt the following climate-related actions? (5-point scale, very easy to very difficult)
- Phasing out exposure to high carbon assets
- Integrating climate change into valuations
- Investing in low carbon opportunities
- Engaging with external fund managers
- Engaging with companies
- Engaging with policy makers and regulators
- Collaborating with other investors
- Undertaking climate change scenario analysis
- Reviewing asset allocation assumptions
- Reviewing governance oversight

10. In your opinion, what are the most important challenges with incorporating climate-related impacts into investment decisions? (5-point scale, not important to very important)
- Lack of comparable data and tools
- It is too far into the future to assess
- High degree of uncertainty
- There are other more pressing issues
- Risk of underperforming peers in short term
- Not standard industry practice
- It does not fit into existing valuation models
- Underperformance versus benchmark
- Lack of time and resources
- Lack of internal buy-in
- High degree of complexity
- Does not fit into team culture

11. In your opinion, what are the risks associated with integrating climate-related impacts into investment decisions? (5-point scale, not a risk to very high risk)
- Underperform peers
- Breach of fiduciary duty

- Short-term underperformance
- Less diversified portfolio
- Too complex to evaluate
- Time and resource intensive
- Distraction from higher priority activities
- Too far into the future to consider
- Not well entrenched across industry
- Hard to defend if it goes wrong
- Losing credibility
- Getting fired/lower bonus

12. In your opinion, what are the risks associated with not integrating climate-related impacts into investment decisions? (5-point scale, not a risk to very high risk)

- Lag peers
- Regulator crackdown
- Breach of fiduciary duty
- Membership/beneficiary pressure
- Reputation risk
- Lose leadership status
- Higher portfolio risk
- Miss out on new opportunities
- Less diversified portfolio
- Higher system-wide costs of climate change
- Weak signal for companies to act
- Weak signal for governments to act

13. Please share any further comments or insights that you may have on investor behaviour and climate change.

Endnotes

[1] https://www.unprme.org/working-group/prme-working-group-on-sustainability-mindset

[2] https://www.clientearth.org/latest/documents/10-landmark-climate-change-cases/

[3] https://www.climateaction100.org

[4] Aristotle 980a Metaphysics, Translated by W. D. Ross.

[5] https://www.climateaction100.org/approach/how-we-got-here/, see for example the Church of England pension fund's decision to divest from Shell, BP and other oil and gas companies after failed attempts to change fossil fuel expansion activities through the CA100+ engagement efforts (of which the fund was a founding member.

[6] See for example https://theinvestoragenda.org; https://www.gfanzero.com/; https://www.climateaction100.org

[7] https://theinvestoragenda.org/wp-content/uploads/2022/08/2022-Global-Investor-Statement-.pdf

[8] See for example the Long Term Investors Club (http://www.ltic.org); and the Focusing Capital on the Long Term initiative (https://www.fcltglobal.org/)

www.ingramcontent.com/pod-product-compliance
Ingram Content Group UK Ltd.
Pitfield, Milton Keynes, MK11 3LW, UK
UKHW041643031026
15587UKWH00001B/463